WITHIN YOU IS
THE POWER

WITHIN YOU IS THE POWER

(Around the World with Dr. Murphy)

JOSEPH MURPHY

D.D., D.R.S., Ph.D., LL.D.

A TARCHERPERIGEE BOOK

tarcherperigee

An imprint of Penguin Random House LLC
375 Hudson Street
New York, New York 10014

Originally published by DeVorss & Company.

Tarcher and Perigee are registered trademarks, and the colophon is
a trademark of Penguin Random House LLC.

Most TarcherPerigee books are available at special quantity discounts for bulk
purchase for sales promotions, premiums, fund-raising, and educational needs.
Special books or book excerpts also can be created to fit specific needs.
For details, write: SpecialMarkets@penguinrandomhouse.com.

Library of Congress Cataloging-in-Publication Data

Names: Murphy, Joseph, 1898-1981, author.
Title: Within you is the power : (around the world with Dr. Murphy) / by
Joseph Murphy, D.D., Ph.D., LL.D., D.R.S.
Description: New York, NY : TarcherPerigee, 2017.
Identifiers: LCCN 2016027003 | ISBN 9780143129868 (paperback)
Subjects: LCSH: Spiritual life—Miscellanea. | Self-actualization (Psychology) |
BISAC: BODY, MIND & SPIRIT / New Thought. | BODY, MIND &
SPIRIT / Inspiration & Personal Growth. | SELF-HELP / Personal Growth / Success.
Classification: LCC BF1999 .M823 2017 | DDC 299/.93—dc23

Printed in the United States of America
1 3 5 7 9 10 8 6 4 2

CONTENTS

Staff They Comfort Me—Thou Preparest a Table Before Me in the Presence of Mine Enemies—Thou Anointest My Head with Oil—My Cup Runneth Over—Surely Goodness and Mercy Shall Follow Me All the Days of My Life—I Will Dwell in the House of the Lord Forever.

1

Within You Is the Power
(Around the World with Dr. Murphy)

I TOOK A 50-day journey around the world in October 1976 with fascinating sightseeing excursions everywhere, visiting Greece, Turkey, Egypt, Jordan, Israel, India, Nepal, Thailand, Singapore, Hong Kong, Japan, and Hawaii. I met many interesting people, visited the various shrines, and heard lectures regarding the various religious beliefs, miraculous healings at shrines, techniques of prayer used, and the unique way of many in approaching the Invisible Presence and Power. During this trip I had the opportunity of talking to many people on the laws of mind and the way of the Spirit. I was intensely interested in knowing that all those people in the many countries visited wanted to hear more about the workings of the subconscious mind.*

One of the reasons for this trip was to gather material for a book. Therefore, I made mental notes of everything I saw

---

* See *The Power of Your Subconscious Mind* by Dr. Joseph Murphy, Prentice-Hall Publishing Company, Englewood Cliffs, New Jersey, 1963.

and heard, much of which will be incorporated in the following pages.

The City of Athens is quite modern with an interest and charm of its own. It becomes more fascinating each time I visit it. Actually, it is a literal exploration of antiquity: The Parthenon, the Temple of Olympic Zeus, and excursions to Eleusis and Corinth. This reminded me of the Eleusinian mysteries and the invitation into all ancient temple mystery rites, which were repositories of ancient spiritual treasures.

You Are Your Own Savior

The guide at Corinth expounded quite extensively on the fact that we were standing on the same spot where Paul stood as he expatiated and descanted on his Epistles to the Corinthians. Then he added that Paul knew that Jesus was man's savior. This is not correct, however, as you will perceive in perusing this chapter. Paul said: . . . *Christ in you, the hope of glory* (Colossians 1:27). *And if Christ be not risen, then is our preaching vain* . . . (I Corinthians 15:14). . . . *Awake thou that sleepest, and arise from the dead, and Christ shall give thee light* (Ephesians 5:14).

What does the Bible mean by such language? The literal interpretation of the Bible has done much towards driving thinking people into unbelief. We must understand that the scriptures of the world abound in symbolisms. Many phrases and chapters of the Bible reveal the impossibility of being rendered literally; and if any part is admitted to be figurative, allegorical, and mystical, so many other parts may be. The men who wrote the Bible, most of whom are nameless, said to themselves: "We know what we wish to convey, but how can we explain it to the people?" Therefore, they decided to speak of problems, difficulties, wars, strife, sickness, etc., and then explained how to overcome the problems of which they spoke.

The Hope of Glory

This is not a sanctimonious state, singing of hymns, going to church, following the rules and tenets of some religious organization, etc. It means the practice of the Presence of God within you. It means to express light, love, truth, and beauty now and to be happy and living in the joyous expectancy of the best. When you are exuding vibrancy and your family and social relationships are good, that is also the glory (the glow and the ray) of God. Christ means the Presence of God in you.

The word "Christ," as you know, is not a proper name. It refers to a title. It is a Greek word meaning anointed or consecrated. It corresponds to the Hebrew word "Messiah" and to the word "Buddha." The Christ in you means the Divine Presence in you, the spiritual truth about you. Jesus is the name of a man. The words "Jesus" and "Joshua" are synonymous. The latter means "God is the solution." God is the salvation or the solution to all your problems. To see Christ in the other means to see (perceive spiritually) peace where there is discord, love where there is hatred, joy where there is sadness, and wholeness, beauty, and perfection where there is sickness. This mental and spiritual exercise is ofttimes referred to as the practice of the Presence of God.

And I, if I be lifted up from the earth, will draw all men unto me (John 12:32). This means that when, through prayer and meditation, you lift your ideal up to the point of acceptance, the manifestation will appear. In other words, you will experience the joy of the answered prayer.

TOUCHING THE DIVINE PRESENCE

When you pray and there follows a sense of peace, quietness, and confidence, that means that you have mentally touched your Higher Self (God in you; the I AM) and that you have begun to know yourself a little better. The Christ in you is "The I AM," the Living Spirit Almighty, the Life Principle. Descartes said, *"Cogito ergo sum,"* which means: "I think; therefore, I AM."

The capacity of Spirit is to think, enabling you to choose, compare, weigh, and decide. You have volition, choice, and initiative. The only immaterial power you are aware of is your thought. Descartes rationalized that all objective evidence is not absolutely true, e.g., optical illusions, others deceiving you, etc. The only sure thing in the universe is that God is God. When you say "I AM," you are announcing the Presence of God within you.

GOD IN ACTION IN YOU

When you are kind and generous and lift up others in your thought and feeling and say something good and uplifting, that's the I AM in you. You are an individualization of Infinite Spirit, and you are here to express more and more of your Divinity. We rise from the dead when we give up old beliefs, superstitions, and false beliefs and awaken to the God-Presence within.

Visit to Istanbul

There was a group of twenty-one on our trip. All were of different religious beliefs, and all of us agreed that we were indeed in an exotic city, which has one foot in Europe and another in Asia. It is worthwhile to view the famous Blue Mosque, the Mosque of Suleyman the Magnificent, the Museum of St. Sophia, and the Hippodrome.

The Turks are probably the most zealous of the Moslems. Friday is the Sabbath of Islam, and business is suspended to some degree. Prayers are read and sermons given by the priests in the mosques. There were many people assembled in the mosques we visited, but the silence was so profound I was unaware that it contained a single worshipper. The essential doctrine is the absolute unity and supremacy of God. Allah is God and Mohammed is His prophet.

A Reasonable Question and the Answer

In chatting with one of the men in the mosque, he asked why we insist that we must accept Jesus as our savior. He then quoted what a missionary had said in the Christian school he attended as a boy: *For God so loved the world, that he gave his only begotten Son, that whosoever believeth in him should not perish, but have everlasting life* (John 3:16).

My explanation was as follows: Some preachers unfortunately take the Bible literally, forgetting the age-old truths: . . . *The letter killeth, but the spirit giveth life* (II Corinthians 3:6). *Call no man your father upon the earth: for one is your Father, which is in heaven* (Matthew 23:9). . . . *I ascend unto my Father, and your Father; and to my God, and your God* (John 20:17). All this indicates that we have a common Father or Progenitor, the Life Principle; and that, in reality, we are all brothers and sisters.

I pointed out to him that every man is his own savior because God indwells all men. The Bible says: *I have said, Ye are gods; and all of you are children of the most High* (Psalm 82:6). Paul says: *For as many as are led by the Spirit of God, they are the sons of God* (Romans 8:14). God is no respecter of persons. *For there is no respect of persons with God* (Romans 2:11).

The Bible is essentially a psychological and spiritual textbook and is not taken literally by vast numbers of people who study the inner meaning of the symbols, parables, fables, myths, cryptograms, and numbers mentioned throughout the volume.

I admitted to him that many clergymen talk about salvation of the soul in afterlife; but tomorrow, next week, next year is afterlife. The Life Principle in each of us is constantly bringing forth on the screen of space the results of our habitual thinking and imagery. Man can't lose his soul, which is eternal and indestructible, any more than God can lose Himself.

There is no lost soul. A man may be lost to harmony, health, and peace from a psychological standpoint; but he can always unite with the Infinite Spirit within him and again claim, feel, and experience that which he thought he had lost. Man wants to be saved from sickness, pain, misery, lack, and suffering here and now. This is the immediate and essential problem—not only in Turkey, but in all other parts of the world.

Man's future is his present thinking objectified as experience and conditions in his life. You do not associate the salvation or solution to your problem with a man or another personality, whether it be Jesus, Mohammed, Buddha, or Laotze. You look to no man to save you. You realize that if you are lost in the jungle, there is no man to save you; but if you turn to the Infinite Intelligence within you, the answer will come and you will be led out to freedom and safety.

"God gave His son," which means His expression, His power, His attributes, and lodged them in the subconscious of every man. This is why Paul says: . . . *That thou stir up the gift of God, which is in thee* . . . (II Timothy 1:6). *Know ye not that ye are the temple of God, and that the Spirit of God dwelleth in you?* (I Corinthians 3:16).

God imaged Himself to be man, and God became what He imagined Himself to be. Every man is a manifestation or the projected image of the Infinite. All the powers of God are in every man. The image-making power is the first faculty of man. Whatever man imagines and feels himself to be, comes to pass for the simple reason that whatever is impressed on the subconscious mind is expressed and made manifest as form, function, experience, and event.

My new acquaintance told me of the truth of the latter statement. He said he had been sickly as a boy, having been born in the slums and grown up depressed and hungry many times. A member of his mosque had told him to imagine he was in college and to look at his degree on the wall every night as though he had it now; and that Allah would bring it to pass. He had practiced this technique every night. One day at the beach he had saved a girl from drowning. Her father, who was an Ambassador, was very grateful and sent him to England to study, paying all his college expenses. He is now experiencing the everlasting life spoken of in that Bible passage.

The word "everlasting" means a continuous life without the great swings of fate; a creative, peaceful, harmonious life without ups and downs, sickness and health, wealth and poverty, depression and joy. He leads a constructive, progressive pattern of life. This is really the meaning of that biblical passage, which is lost in theological complexities and which becomes an absurdity to the reasoning mind. Moreover, it is really an insult to the Jew, the Moslem, the Buddhist, and the Shintoist to tell him he has to believe in the personality of Jesus to be saved. Saved from what? We need to be saved from ignorance, fear, superstition, poverty, and disease. Ignorance is the only sin, and all the suffering is the consequence.

GET A NEW CONCEPTION OF YOURSELF

God is the Universal Presence and Power, instantly available to all men regardless of whether they are atheists, agnostics, or holy men. Your thought is creative. You can begin to get a new self-image of being what you long to be. Nourish that image with faith and confidence and you will discover that the creative Power of God is within you. Then you will know for the first time that you are your own savior, and it will prove to you that God indwells you.

There is only one Creative Power. See this clearly. Reason it out until it becomes a conviction within you beyond all argument, disputation, or dialectics, in which you rest mentally in peace and harmony. All the wisdom and power of God are within you as the only begotten Son of God, which means the expression, the offspring, the projection of the Infinite Spirit in you. We are all begotten of the Only One, for there is only One Presence and Power. The above explanation completely satisfied my Moslem friend, and he is now reading *The Power of Your Subconscious Mind** and *Peace Within Yourself.*†

THE LAND OF THE PHARAOHS

This was my third visit to this fascinating area. One is carried back in time when he visits Luxor and sees the glorious Temple of Karnak, the Valley of the Kings, and the Colossi of Memnon in Thebes, sights that really fill all visitors with a sort of mystic awe and wonder. We heard lectures in the Egyptian museum in Cairo, and viewed the fabulous relics taken from King Tutankhamun's tomb, the Alabaster Sphinx and the Great Pyramid of Cheops. There was also a thrilling Sound and Light Spectacle at the Pyramids depicting the fabulous days of the Pharaohs.

---

* *The Power of Your Subconscious Mind* by Dr. Joseph Murphy, Prentice-Hall Publishing Co., Englewood Cliffs, N.J., 1963.
† *Peace Within Yourself* by Dr. Joseph Murphy, DeVorss and Company, Inc., Marina del Rey, California, 1956.

THE GREAT PYRAMID

This Pyramid is referred to as the chief of the Seven Wonders of the World and many times is called a "gospel in stone." It is at the center of the universe, symbolizing the great truth that God is at the center of your being. The Pyramid refers to man and the universe. Scientists from all over the world have studied its marvelous structure, its vast age and exquisite workmanship, and the mystery of its origin. Our lecturer on the Pyramids pointed out to us that distinguished astronomers, mathematicians, Egyptologists, and archaeologists have conducted extensive research and have concluded that the original designers were men of a very high intelligence and possessed of cosmic wisdom.

THE FOUR CARDINAL POINTS—THE WAY OF PRAYER

The orientation of the Great Pyramid relates to the four cardinal points of the compass, which symbolize the four parts of man: spiritual, mental, emotional, and physical. The four cardinal points also refer to the four letters in the name Jehovah, i.e., Yod-He-Vau-He. Yod is Consciousness, Spirit, I AM. He is the idea, the thought-image in your mind. Vau represents feeling, love, and emotion. The final He is the manifestation of that which you imaged and felt to be true. This is the way all things are made. There is nothing made that is not made this way. God speaks to you through desire. Feel the reality of your desire, nourish it, sustain it, imagine the reality of it, see the happy ending, and gradually it will gel in your subconscious mind and come to pass.

Your Diameter Determines Your Future

The Pyramid, which is also a story of man, portrays the relationship of the diameter to the circumference of the circle, which is expressed in numerical values. The circle represents Infinity, or God, which has no beginning and no end. The diameter determines the circumference of the circle. The diameter is your concept, your estimate or blueprint of yourself, which determines the circle of your acquaintances, your social, political, financial, and professional status in your world. You can always enlarge the diameter and build a greater self-image, thereby magnifying and enlarging your inner potential, enabling you to serve humanity in a greater way and prosper along all lines.

She Drew a Larger Diameter

While conversing with a retired musician, she told me that she was bored in retirement and so one day sat down quietly and affirmed: "God magnifies my talents in a wonderful way, and more and more people are blessed by what I offer." Professors, teachers, ministers, and college students have flocked to her for private tuition. Actually, she has to turn some away, as she can't handle them all. She has discovered the *élan* of life, the joy of giving of her talents and releasing the imprisoned splendor within. She has discovered that age is not the flight of years but is instead the dawn of wisdom.

THE INTERPRETATION OF PYRAMID

Various interpretations have been given to the word "pyramid," such as "light of the sun." The real meaning is "measure of ten." The number of corners and sides added equals ten. The numeral ten means, from a phallic standpoint, the male and female generative organs, which symbolically means the union of the male and female principle in all of us. Therefore, the real meaning of the Pyramid is the interaction of your conscious and subconscious mind, the harmonious union of which brings forth harmony, health, peace, and abundance in your life. The King's Chamber and the Queen's Chamber represent the male and female principle in all of us.

THE FIRST-YEAR FRUITS

A rancher who accompanied us asked me: "Why are the first fruits given to the Lord?" He quoted this passage: . . . *Thou shalt take of the first of all the fruit of the earth, which thou shalt bring of thy land that the Lord thy God giveth thee, and shalt put it in a basket* . . . (Deuteronomy 26:2).

There is a custom among many people in the Middle East and other places to let the first fruits die, as they belong to God. The first born, according to the traditions of Israel, gets the property or estate. There is the law of primogeniture in some countries, which is seniority by birth in a family having the same father and mother. In English law, it is the exclusive right of inheritance belonging to a first-born son.

The law of life is a reversal of all this. To reject the first fruits and eat only those that follow is all due to misunderstanding. The explanation is simple. All it means is this: That which you now are and that which you long to be. You must die to the old state and live to the new. In other words, you exalt and nourish the ideal in your mind, knowing that an Almighty Power is moving on your behalf. As you remain faithful to your ideal, it will gel within you and the old state dies and the new manifestation appears.

She Said: "Everything Is Going Backwards"

A woman asked me: "Why do I have all these problems? I have prayed for a new state. I know what I want, but everything is going backwards." I explained to her that her prayer process was changing her subconscious mind, and as she continued to take her attention away from the old state, it would gradually disintegrate, and the process of change might be somewhat annoying. When you sweep the room out, it makes dust and you wish to leave the room. But when it is clean, you sit down and everything is satisfactory. You don't see the dust. Nine times out of ten, this happens. As you fill your subconscious with life-giving patterns, the old derelicts and complexes hidden in the subconscious put up a fight, creating a little dust; but as you continue the cleansing process, your whole world changes and you are transformed.

SHE WANTED A FUR COAT

I chatted with a woman on the tour who told me that some years previously she had wanted a fur coat but did not have the money to buy one. Winter was approaching in New York City, where the temperature becomes very low. She had been picturing herself wearing a mink coat, feeling the reality of it, touching the imaginary coat, and in her imagination looking at herself in the mirror while wearing it and feeling the joy of it. Some days later she went into Macy's to look over coats for sale and try them on. In the meantime, however, her old coat was stolen and the management gave her a mink coat at a very reduced price which at the time she was able to afford.

Her subconscious mind arranged all this in its own way. It knows all and does not have to reason things out. Infinite Intelligence dwells therein. If you reason inductively, you admit that all things are not possible. The woman mentioned above reasoned that she could not afford a mink coat; but, picturing one on her and feeling the reality of it, her subconscious accepted her desire and brought it to pass in its own way. All things are possible to your deeper mind. Undoubtedly, the above-mentioned woman had succeeded by constant imaging in impregnating her subconscious mind, which responded according to the image in her mind.

MAN HAS CHOICE

You can choose to be successful, happy, joyous, and free. The part is not written for you. There is no predestination. If so, we would have no right to criticize anyone or commend anyone in the world, as they would simply be fulfilling a role as an actor in a play. You can play any role you wish by stirring up the gift of God within you. You must remember that we could not awaken that within us unless it were already there in the first place. There is merit when you say that your boy has chosen the good. *For a thousand years in thy sight are but as yesterday when it is past, and as a watch in the night* (Psalm 90:4). This is a poetic expression meaning a million years are as a second in the drama of awakening. Let the resurrection of God's powers take place in you, and wonders will happen as you pray.

2

Cease Blaming Your Parents

JORDAN IS A fascinating country, and a trip to Petra reveals a magnificent rose-red city of ancient rock-hewn palaces, tombs, temples, stairs, and streets. The visitor is seized with a sort of mystic awe while wandering through the ancient ruins of this historic city. Several excavations at the site of the biblical Dibon have revealed that occupation of the site goes back to the early Bronze Age, about 3000 B.C.

While conversing with a man in the hotel at Amman, capital of Jordan, he told me that he had never known his parents, had been born in the slums, and now was a diplomat attached to a foreign embassy. He was on vacation visiting some of the historic sites of his homeland. While talking he brought up a great truth which was that no matter what the origin of your birth, you can rise, transcend, and grow if you know how to contact the Divine Presence within, Which knows all and sees all.

He said that many scientists and fiction writers claim that

our genes determine our destiny and that all they have to do in the future is change the genetic code; then we can bring forth the type of men and women we want in the world, just about the same as we breed cattle or pedigreed horses. He added laughingly that some point out that if a woman wants a child like Einstein, Lincoln, Paderewski, Carver, or some other great statesman or scholar, all she would have to do, provided there was a frozen spermatic fluid bank of the particular man she wanted, would be to have artificial insemination; then she could give birth to the type of man she admired. Others say that all we have to do is get some cells from a distinguished man and then place them in a culture media and we could duplicate as many of that type man we would wish. There is much folderol and balderdash plus fiction in all of this.

It is true, of course, that we inherit through the genes the color of our eyes, hair, skin, and many other characteristics. We are told that we also inherit the inclination to acquire certain diseases and that stupidity and a high intelligence quotient are passed on to us by our parents. It is time that we ask ourselves, however, what we have inherited from the Infinite Presence and Power of God within us. Actually, we are temples of the Living God, and we are here to reveal all the powers, attributes, and qualities of God inherent within us.

Think of it this way: You were a boy who had a father, who was a boy, who had a father. Keep on going back. Where does it lead you? Back to the primordial cell, the Divine Source, the Father of all. All religions say "Our Father." All of us have a common progenitor, the Life Principle. The genes of Abraham, Moses, Jesus, Elijah, Mohammed, etc., are all within us.

So are the genes of Genghis Khan, Socrates, Plato, and Aristotle. If you are a native American, ponder over all the ancestors you have had since the pilgrims landed. A mathematician could figure it out for you quickly. Robby Wright, a young physicist whose lineage goes back to the early sixteenth century, figured he had 17,000 ancestors since 1600.

You Are Not a Victim of Heredity

A sister of mine, who taught school for many years prior to her entry into the Convent in England, told me that she once had a very bright boy in her class. Actually, he excelled all the others, and she recommended him to the local priest, who agreed to send him to the Seminary. Tuition would be free. However, he refused. His reason was: "I am only a miner's son." His father had the same attitude. This attitude of mind held him and other boys like him in bondage.

There is an interesting sequel to this. A member of the local gentry wanted to adopt a boy. My sister recommended a child in an orphanage nearby, whose parents were dead. This man and his wife adopted the boy at once, completely indifferent to the fact that for several generations his progenitors had been miners. This boy received private education by a governess and later on was sent to a college in England. He grew up according to the standards of the day and associated only with wealthy boys and girls. He followed the customs and traditions and the caste system which prevailed in his upbringing and environmental training. On one of his visits home, he called on my sister to invite her to his birthday party and mentioned that he could not invite the student who was going to drive her to the party because he was a miner's son.

You can see the whole picture: an orphan boy, a miner's son, conditioned, educated, and trained to have a high estimate of himself, who, because of his training, thought another miner's son inferior. The other boy mentioned previously, who was so brilliant, lacked the heart to try because he was taught to think he was of a lower class and considered himself inferior. His mental attitude held him back—not his genes, chromosomes, or the fact he was a miner's son.

CONSIDER THE SOURCE

It is foolish to look to your parents, grandparents, or ancestors as the source of your powers, qualities, tendencies, aptitudes, and characteristics. You thereby limit your potential. Realize that you came from God. God indwells you and is your Heavenly Father. All His wisdom, power, and glory are at your disposal, waiting for you to call on His inexhaustible reservoir of strength and intelligence. You are not a mere confluence of atoms, molecules, genes, and inherited tendencies. Instead, you are a son of the Living God and heir to all of God's riches—spiritual, mental, and material.

And be not conformed to this world: but be ye transformed by the renewing of your mind, that ye may prove what is that good, and acceptable, and perfect, will of God (Romans 12:2). This is the key to a new life. Your mind is a recording machine, and all the theological beliefs, impressions, opinions, and ideas accepted by you and given to you in your childhood are impressed in your subconscious mind.

But you can change your mind. You can begin to fill your mind now with God-like patterns of thoughts and align yourself with the Infinite Spirit within you, claiming beauty, love, peace, joy, wisdom, power, and creative ideas. The Spirit in you will respond, transforming your mind, body, and circumstances. Your thought is the medium between Spirit and your body and the material world.

THE NEW RACE OF MEN AND WOMEN

Great men and women will not come forth in this country because their ancestors came over on the Mayflower or because of their heredity, or by those who think you can bring forth a better race of people somewhat similar to the way you breed horses. You can't omit Spirit or God. Some of the greatest minds came out of the slums. George Carver looked to the Spirit within him for guidance and inspiration, and he rose to the heights and blessed his people and his country through his discoveries, inventions, and formulas as a great chemist. He ceased to think of himself as a slave or a serf or as inferior to anyone.

His constant prayer was: *In all thy ways acknowledge him, and he shall direct thy paths* (Proverbs 3:6). And God answered him, blessed him, and prospered him. Ask yourself frequently: What did I inherit from the Infinite? And the answer is: All of God indwells me, and I must acknowledge this

Power and awaken this Presence within me and bring forth wonders, for His name is Wonderful.

He Was Born in Hell's Kitchen

One of the great surgeons I knew once told me that he had been born in Hell's Kitchen; that his mother was a prostitute; that he was taught to steal when young; and that he never even knew his father. You might say that everything was against him or ask what chance he had. The answer is that he had the chance of a lifetime. One day a surgeon dressed his wound following a fight, and he said that the man was so kind and good to him that he decided to become a surgeon himself.

He related the following: "I held a picture of myself dressed in white, operating, and I asked God to help me. Suddenly a change came over me. I could not steal any more. I studied hard, won a scholarship, and one of the professors paid all my expenses in medical school, saying, 'You can pay me back by becoming a good doctor and a good surgeon.'" God had answered his prayer.

Revealing Your Divinity

We can bring about changes in cellular structure of cactus, corn, rice, and fruits, as scientists are doing from day to day. In order to bring forth a more God-like man or woman, however, it does not depend on his or her body or structure of the brain; it depends entirely on stirring up the invisible, the intangible powers of God within. You do not mix in a mortar qualities such as honesty, integrity, justice, joy, courage, faith, confidence, inspiration, love, and goodwill. You can't incorporate dreams, visions, and illumination in some mixture and say, "Now, we will have a new man." Character is destiny.

In order to transcend, man will need peace. That inner peace will enable him to be at peace with the world. He will need love and goodwill to overcome the anger, trials, and tribulations of the world. He will need courage, faith, and confidence in the creative laws of his mind, causing him to serve the rest of mankind in a more wonderful way and bring peace to this changing world. Peace, harmony, joy, love, wisdom, and understanding are of God. You can't build these into a man or woman, since they are already there, only waiting to be released by the individual.

> *Wherefore I put thee in remembrance that thou stir up the gift of God, which is in thee* . . . (II Timothy 1:6).

WHO ARE YOUR CHILDREN?

Gibran, the mystic poet, points out: "Your children come through you, but not by you." *And call no man your father upon the earth: for one is your Father, which is in heaven* (Matthew 23:9).

You come from a noble lineage when you contemplate your Father, or God, or this Invisible Presence and Power Which created all things, visible and invisible. Heaven means the Infinite Intelligence in which you live, move, and have your being. When you pray, go back to the Source of all Life and claim guidance, wisdom, abundance, and inspiration from the Pristine Presence within—the Father of all.

Refuse to give power to conditions, circumstances, events, or to the genetic records of parents, grandparents, or all the ancestors who preceded you. Men, women, and conditions are not the cause of your good fortune or misfortune. The Supreme Cause—the only Cause and Power—is Spirit. You are not bound by karma or the past. God indwells you. Rejoice and be glad and grow tall in wisdom, truth, and beauty.

Let God Arise in You

Lincoln failed many times in his political career, but he kept on persisting, having faith and confidence in a Supreme Power to lead him and guide him. He did not look at his so-called handicaps. He walked 40 miles to hear a lecture. His parents were illiterate and extremely poor, but he had a vision; and, through the power of God, he fulfilled it.

Beethoven was deaf, but he heard the music of the spheres with an inner ear. Leonardo da Vinci came from an impoverished background and was the son of a country girl and a local philanderer. Edison was kicked out of a school because the teacher said he was too backward, but he decided nevertheless to light up the world. Einstein was rejected by several schools, because he was considered not bright enough to be admitted, but he nevertheless went forth and touched the heights in mathematics and physics and revealed a world of

Divine law and order. Newton was the son of a very poor farmer who died before he was born. Newton turned to the Source of all wisdom, and he gave us the law of action and reaction, lighting up the minds of men with his astronomical deductions and discoveries.

Realize that genius springs from the poorest of families. Milton, though blind, gave us *Paradise Lost*. Divine imagination was Milton's spiritual eye, which enabled him to go about God's business, whereby he annihilated time, space, and matter and brought forth the truths of the Invisible Presence within all of us. Remember how Chico, the Parisian sewer cleaner, imagined and lived in a paradisiacal state of mind called the "seventh heaven" even though he never saw the light of day.

Being born in a palace, or being a king's son or a scion of a noble family does not necessarily mean we will have another Milton, Shakespeare, Phidias, or Beethoven. Men accomplish great things when they become conscious of Divine lineage and in quiet moments of meditation and Divine imagery become aware of the fact that the invisible things of Him from the foundation of time are clearly visible.

FAITH IS YOUR INNER AWARENESS

Your mental attitude represents your faith. According to your faith in the Creative Intelligence within you is it done unto you. Become aware of the guidance and goodness of the Infinite operating in you, through you, and all around you.

Eradicate Alibis and Excuses

Some years ago I read where an attorney pleaded excuses for the vicious criminal acts of his client by stating that the man came from an impoverished family and squalid environment; that his father was a drunkard and his mother followed the primrose path. The wise judge said to him, "Don't give me that story. This man's brother, brought up in the same area under the same environmental conditions, is one of our most distinguished jurists in the state."

The butterfly comes forth from the cocoon and develops wings, enabling it to fly and reveal its beauty and glory. Likewise, you can come forth from your house or prison of limitation or bondage and soar aloft with the wings of faith and imagination and so reveal your own glory.

Your Divine Parentage and Human Parentage

It is true that you inherited from your parents certain genetic tendencies which determine the color of your skin and eyes and your physical constitution. Your temperament and disposition are affected by the mental and emotional atmosphere of the home. Every child is subject to the early training, indoctrination, moods, feelings, and beliefs of the parents. However, when the child grows up and becomes aware of the Divine Presence within, he can rise and transcend any handicap. Suddenly he becomes aware of his Divine Source. As he begins to contemplate the eternal verities, he is lifted up above the parental and environmental atmosphere and influence, both past and present.

OUR CONDITIONING AND TRAINING

We may have been victims of false teaching, false theological beliefs about God, life, and the universe; but we can change the negative beliefs by making it a habit to regularly think constructively, harmoniously, and peacefully. Our subconscious is the seat of habit, but we should be aware that all habits can be changed. Our mental and emotional fears, superstitions, taboos, and strictures were undoubtedly transferred to us in our youth.

During my tour of India, Nepal, Thailand, and other countries, I heard college graduates say to me, "Oh! I may come back in another life as a tiger, lion, dog, or other animal if I don't behave in this life." They mentioned that their present status in life was based on their karma, and that they were reaping what they had sown in a former life. They believed they were being punished for past wrong doing. To many of them, karma was a cruel law which imposed punishment upon them, a sort of eye for an eye and tooth for a tooth.

All this is far from the truth. Regardless of man's past, if met in the right way, Divine love dissolves everything unlike Itself. God is the Eternal Now. Karma means the law of action and reaction. In the Mind-Principle there is no time or space. Any man can transform his life now by giving himself a Divine transfusion of love, light, and truth. He wipes out the consequences of past errors through the cleansing of his subconscious mind. When we pollute or impress false beliefs in our subconscious mind, we suffer the consequences; or we can eradicate them by scientific prayer, which is the practice of the Presence of God.

The crimes, errors, mistakes, and heinous offenses of man can be expunged from the subconscious mind, banishing and freeing the person from the results or punishment naturally accruing to the impressions made in the subconscious. Perfunctory prayer or joining some church will not do this. Nothing superficial will suffice; but an intense desire and a real hunger and thirst on the part of the individual for a new birth in God, which alters fundamentally his character, plus a constant saturation of his mind with eternal verities, will wipe out the punishment or reaction from the subconscious.

The action is of the conscious mind and the reaction is that of the subconscious mind. Karma is not some dread sentence to be overcome or which has to be expiated. The idea of karma comes from the East; but in all sacred writings, including the Bhagavad-Gita, you will find that if you return to the Divine Center and contemplate the Truths of God, that is the end of the old state and the birth of the new. All adversity is redemptive and remedial through the practice of the Presence of God. A changed attitude changes everything.

Do the Dead Govern You?

Do the dead thoughts, beliefs, and opinions of people long since gone from this dimension of life govern you? Dead thoughts mean thoughts which are based on ignorance, fear, and superstition. You will find all over the world that millions of people are still governed and driven by tendencies and emotions, such as fear, resentment, greed, hostility, and self-condemnation, all of which are derived from generations long since gone to the next dimension of life.

Remember that all you have been taught and acquired in infancy, even though you may imitate the habits of your parents or grandparents, can be changed by scientific prayer. It stands to reason that the Infinite Intelligence Which created you from a cell can also heal you. It made all your organs and It controls all the vital processes of your body. Your mind is God's mind, as there is but one mind common to all individual men. Tremendous possibilities lie dormant within you.

Your subconscious assumptions, beliefs, and convictions dictate and control all your conscious actions. In other words, you are belief expressed. Come to a decision now and realize you will no longer be subject to the false patterns of thought given to you when young. Spirit, or God, in you is the only Presence, Power, Cause, and Substance. Join up with your Heavenly Father and transform your life.

Spirit and Matter

Modern science knows that Spirit and matter are interconvertible and interchangeable; that matter is simply Spirit slowed down to the point of visibility. It is wrong to say that you are conditioned by your environment—your home, your job, your business, your surroundings—as it is suggestive only; but if accepted by you, you will continue to repeat the same old patterns as your forebears and perhaps live the same old life based on creeds, dogma, and tradition. Externals are not creative. The Creative Power is in you. A scientific thinker does not make a created thing a cause; it is an effect. Knowing the location of the Creative Power and the Primal Cause, you will no longer attribute to any person, place, or situation the power of creation or generation. Your own thought is the only creative power of which you are aware.

Become a Channel for the Divine

Dormant and inherent within you are all the powers of the Infinite. A wonderful prayer to practice is as follows: "God is, and His Holy Presence flows through me as beauty, harmony, love, joy, wisdom, understanding, Divine guidance, and abundance. I know it is just as easy for God to become all these things as it is a blade of grass, and I give thanks that it is so."

Reiterate these truths three or four times night and morning, making sure that you do not subsequently deny what you affirm; and you will find that you really are a son or a daughter of the Infinite and a child of Eternity. All the Powers of the Infinite begin to move through you, which is called in the Bible the Christ in you—the hope of glory. Look always to your spiritual inheritance and never to your human parents or ancestors. You have power over your life and the means and capacity to transform your world.

CEASE BLAMING YOUR PARENTS

As children, all of us were impressionable, malleable, and subject to the beliefs, thoughts, and conditioning of our parents. We did not possess the spiritual understanding or reasoning to reject all the negative thoughts and fears given to us. As an adult, you are responsible for the way you think, feel, believe, and act. You are the only thinker in your world. You and you alone are completely responsible for the way in which you act and react. You are what you think all day long. As you think and feel, so are you and so do you become.

Whatever you were taught by theologians, parents, uncles, aunts, or teachers can be unlearned. The beliefs and traditional concepts you acquired when young, or the mere fact you imitated the superstitious acts of your grandfather when you were eight years old, can all be changed and rectified now, this very moment. Fill your mind with the truths of God and you will then crowd out of your mind everything unlike God.

YOU ARE A KING

It is time for you to claim your kingship because you are a king over your entire conceptive realm. Remember, you could go into the jungles of some country and adopt a boy who is primitive and illiterate and then teach him the wisdom of God and have him practice right thought, right feeling, and right action, while all the time reminding him that he is the son of a king and heir to the throne, and the boy will believe you. He will play the role of a prince. He will develop a regal bearing and a noble stance. Gradually he will become a king over his thoughts, words, deeds, actions, and reactions and assume his sovereignty over his life. This happens because the Almighty King is within him; otherwise, it could never happen.

You are a son of the Living God. Claim your inheritance now. The Inner Voice will say to such a person: . . . *Thou art my son, this day have I begotten thee* . . . (Hebrews 1:5).

3

Do the Constellations Govern You?

Ideas for this chapter came to the author as we took an interesting motorcade ride through Jordan into Israel, crossing the Allenby Bridge and the River Jordan. We took a sightseeing tour of the famous religious shrines so popular in the stories in the Bible.

A visit to Bethlehem is intensely interesting, as is viewing the lovely hills and valleys of Judea en route. The monastery of Elijah and the Tomb of Rachel have deep inner meanings. The Mount of Olives means a high state of consciousness as you contemplate things Divine. The Garden of Gethsemane, from an esoteric standpoint, means your own mind where, in deep meditation on the Divine Presence, you press out the oil of joy and experience a moment that lasts forever.

The Wailing Wall reminds us to forget the things that are behind and to press towards the mark for the prize of wisdom, truth, beauty, and joy now. St. Stephen's Church and the Dome of the Rock remind us that the church is really within us and that we are here to draw out the wonders of the Infinite within us. Church means "ecclesia," to draw out the power and wisdom of God from your Higher Self. The rock means your conviction of God's Presence, which is invulnerable, invincible, and impregnable.

Bethany, Lazarus's Tomb and Jericho also have profound inner meanings. Jericho means the fragrant state. When you experience an answer to your prayer, you cannot suppress the joy which arises any more than you can suppress the perfume of the rose. Lazarus's Tomb represents any dead state such as sickness, frustration, and dead ideals or desires which have not been resurrected. When you awaken to your Divine Powers, you will call on the Infinite and resurrect that desire dormant within you. Whatever you claim and feel to be true, your subconscious will resurrect and project onto the screen of space.

The Dead Sea also has its symbolic meaning: Nothing lives in it. It has an inlet but no outlet; that is why it is dead. This is to teach us to give generously and joyously of our talents, abilities, and capacities. You can give out cordiality, geniality, and goodwill. You can exude vibrancy and exalt the Divinity in all those around you. Give of God's ideas. Give as the tree gives its fruit and the sun gives its rays, and ask no questions. Let there be a Divine circulation of God's love, peace, and harmony always operating in you. Let your wealth circulate wisely, judiciously, and constructively. All this is essential for a full and happy life. It is natural to give love in the same manner as a mother gives love to the baby in the cradle. She does not exact a quid pro quo.

Bethlehem means the house of bread; i.e., the bread of peace, harmony, joy, inspiration, and Divine guidance. This is the bread of life. Bethany means the overcoming of any problem through the Power of God in you. Elijah means the Presence of God, or the awareness of the I AM in you, and the knowledge that the indwelling God is your savior.

HE BLAMED THE STARS

"There is a malefic configuration of the planets in my horoscope, and everything is going wrong. Saturn is square my Sun sign," announced a man who came to consult me some time ago. He was convinced that his acute loss of vision and financial losses were preordained by the stars, even though his ophthalmologist, after examining the fundus of his eye, felt that most likely an emotional disturbance was the source of his declining vision. I might add that he was intensely jealous of the financial success of an associate in business, which was the real reason for his pecuniary embarrassment and ailing ventures.

I explained to this man that it is well known in psychosomatic medicine today that mental and emotional factors play a definite role in disease. During my consultation with this man, who was so afraid of his horoscope, he revealed that he was deeply resentful and full of hostility towards his mother-in-law. He said that he actually hated the sight of her.

I explained to him that his subconscious mind takes him literally and that it selected his eyes as the scapegoat. Furthermore, his jealousy of an associate's financial success brought impoverishment to himself, because, in effect, he was saying to himself, "He can succeed and go up the ladder and be wealthy, and I can't." He was, in effect, placing the other on a pedestal and demoting himself. Actually, he was stealing from himself and attracting more lack, misery, and limitation to himself.

The realization of what he was doing to himself became the cure. He requested his mother-in-law to move, which she did. His resentment and hostility disappeared as he affirmed freely and lovingly: "I radiate love and goodwill to you, and I wish you all the blessings of life. I see the Presence of God operating in you, through you, and all around you."

He made a habit of this prayer, and his vision subsequently returned to normal. His ophthalmologist informed him that his vision was normal. As a matter of fact, he had been decreeing his own blindness, since his subconscious had no alternative other than to obey his conscious mind's directives. He began to pray for the success and prosperity of his associate and, much to his amazement, he began to prosper again. He discovered that in praying for the success and prosperity of the man of whom he was jealous, he was also praying for himself. This new attitude of mind dissolved all jealousy, which is the child of fear. All this happened despite the extensive foreboding of the astrological charts.

THE ONLY POWER

Shakespeare said, "It is not in our stars but in ourselves that we are underlings." The only power is in your Consciousness, which means the I AM, your Awareness, the Living Spirit, or God, within you. Therefore, you should give allegiance not to the stars, but to the God Which made the stars as well as the planets. We must give power to the Creator; not to the created thing.

It is continually stated in the Bible that we must cease worshipping false gods. *Thou shalt have no other gods before me* (Exodus 20:3). *I am the Lord: that is my name: and my glory will I not give to another, neither my praise to graven images* (Isaiah 42:8). *Thou art wearied in the multitude of thy counsels. Let now the astrologers, the stargazers, the monthly prognosticators, stand up, and save thee from these things that shall come upon thee* (Isaiah 47:13).

THE LAW OF MIND IN ACTION

Two professors who are friends of mine had their astrological charts done for the price of $50 each. At my suggestion, they agreed not to read them lest they impregnate their subconscious mind with the horoscope's negative suggestions. As a matter of fact, for twelve months I was the custodian of their two horoscopes.

During this time I thoroughly explained the law of life to them: *For as he thinketh in his heart, so is he . . .* (Proverbs 23:7). This means that whatever you claim and feel to be true will impregnate the subconscious mind, and whatever is impressed upon the subconscious is eventually expressed. I also explained to them that it is impossible for anything to happen to anyone unless it already has an affinity or some equivalency in the mind. Everyone molds, shapes, and fashions his own destiny by his habitual thought and feeling.

I also explained that even though their subconscious minds may have been polluted with negativity and false beliefs, they could both change by now identifying with the eternal verities rather than with the patterns of the Zodiac. They could charge their mental and spiritual batteries regularly and systematically by contemplating the truths of God, which transcend all the astrological charts.

Each of my friends practiced constructive thinking according to the unchanging principle of the Truth. Finally, at the end of the year, each one examined his horoscope in my office and laughed out loud. There were negative predictions contained in each horoscope which had never come to pass. In fact, where financial losses and accidents were indicated, success and health were encountered instead. Each had not only prospered but had been promoted in his respective college.

Had they read their horoscopes in advance, the negative suggestions would have been impressed upon their subconscious and, undoubtedly, all the things predicted would have occurred. . . . *As thou hast believed, so be it done unto thee* . . . (Matthew 8:13). If you believe in negative predictions, that is what you will, of course, experience, because the law of life is the law of belief.

THE SEARCH

According to the law of allegory, Abraham left Chaldea in search of the true god. The Chaldeans were active in the elaboration of astrology, and they ascribed everything to the movement of the stars, thus profanely likening the created thing to the Creator. Abraham, which means "the Father of the multitude" (Our Father), realized that the world is governed by its Maker and First Cause; and he gave all allegiance to God, the only Presence, Power, Cause, and Substance.

THE PSYCHOLOGY OF ANTIQUITY

Astrology can also be understood as the psychology of antiquity. I have known sensitives and psychics who read the past, the present, and the future with extraordinary acumen, revealing tendencies, and characteristics of individuals, without any knowledge of astrology. Some used a deck of cards and made predictions with amazing accuracy; others, using numbers, revealed past episodes and present plans and purposes. The whole process of the psychic is simply that of tapping the subconscious of the person. The sensitive or psychic is *en rapport* or in touch with your subconscious. Actually, you have told her everything before she tells you anything.

And if there is any validity at all to astrological predictions, it is not because you were born on August 5 or July 4 that you have certain characteristics; rather, it is a result of the collective unconscious beliefs of the race or mass mind regarding that period of the year.

The late Carl Jung said: "Insofar as there are any really correct astrological deductions, they are not due to the effects of the constellations but to our hypothetical time-character."*

---

* See Commentary by Carl Jung on *The Secrets of the Golden Flower*, page 143, Routledge & Kegan Paul, Ltd., Broadway House, London, England, 1931.

In other words, whatever is born or done at this moment of time has the qualities of this moment of time.

This is similar to the operation of the I Ching* of China in which Carl Jung points out in his Foreword that whatever happens in a given moment possesses inevitably the quality peculiar to that moment. Down through the ages the race mind has given power to the constellations and signs, believing that they exert an influence over us. In other words, the whole idea of the influence of the signs under which we were born is based on the collective idea or belief in the subconscious of the race.

All of us are a part of the mass mind or race mind and are affected by the beliefs of the collective unconscious unless we can free our minds through scientific prayer, which means the contemplation of the Truths of God from the highest standpoint. The law is: We become what we contemplate.

MASS MIND BELIEF IN AMERICA

For example, within the subconscious of 200 million people in this country is the superstition or mass mind belief that a president will die or meet an untimely end every twenty years. This does not have to happen, however. If the occupant of the White House saturated his mind with the inner meaning of the 91st Psalm, he would become completely immunized and so God-intoxicated that nothing could touch him.

---

* See *Secrets of the I Ching* by Joseph Murphy, Parker Publishing Co., Inc., West Nyack, N.Y., 1970, and *I CHING*, translated by Wilhelm/Baynes, Princeton University Press, Princeton, N.J., 1967.

How Taurus Becomes Aries

If you say you were born in Taurus when the sun was tropically in that sign, actually, in the sidereal Zodiac based on fixed stars, which is used in the East, the sun would be in Aries. All the delineations you read about are derived from empirical observations. Suppose you were born May 10. An astrologer in India, using the sidereal version of the Zodiac, would say the sun would be in Aries. Consequently, the description of tendencies and characteristics would be different than of someone classifying you as born in Taurus based on outlines given in the various textbooks under that particular sign.

However, when both of the astrologers, forgetting the labels *Aries* and *Taurus*, analyze you according to the period of time, i.e., your date of birth, they would then base their findings on the mass mind belief and empirical observation of thousands of samples taken over the years and would, in all probability, be very similar in their observations and deductions.

Along the same lines, a good graphologist can look at your handwriting and give an excellent delineation of your characteristics, tendencies, aptitudes, and predictions of future successes, etc. All this, again, is based on empirical observations regarding the style of writing and shape of letters, plus the intuitive or psychic perception of the operator.

The Zodiac, with its twelve signs, symbolizes the twelve tribes of the Old Testament and the twelve apostles of the New Testament. In other words, the twelve powers or attributes and qualities of God are within you.

THE NAMES OF STARS

"The ancients," said Maimonides, "directing all their attention to agriculture, gave names to the stars derived from their occupation during the year." To understand astrology in terms of the historical development, the distinguished scholar, C. F. Volney, in *Revolutions of Empires*,* published in English in Paris in 1802, pointed out that it was on the border of the upper Nile, among a race of black men, that the complicated system of the worship of stars was organized. It was considered in relation to the productions of the earth and to the labors of agriculture.

Thus, the Ethiopians named stars of inundation, or Aquarius, those stars under which the Nile began to overflow; stars of the ox or the bull, those stars under which they began to plow; stars of the lion, those under which that animal, driven from the desert by thirst, appeared on the banks of the Nile; stars of the sheaf or of the harvest virgin, those of the reaping season; and stars of the lamb and stars of the two kids, those under which these animals were brought forth.

Thus, the same Ethiopians, having observed that the return of the inundation always corresponded with the rising of the beautiful stars which appeared toward the source of the Nile and seemed to warn the husbandman against the coming waters, compared this action to that of the animal who, by his barking, gives notice of danger, and he called this star, the dog, the barker (Sirius).

---

* See *The Ruins, or, Revolutions of Empires*, by C. F. Volney, Peter Eckler Publishing Co., New York, 1926.

In the same manner, he named the stars of the crab, those where the sun, having arrived at the Tropic, retreated by a slow retrograde motion like the crab, or Cancer. He named stars of the wild goat, or Capricorn, those where the sun, having reached the highest point in its annuary tract, rests at the summit of the horary gnomon, and imitates the goat, who delights in climbing to the summit of the rocks. He names stars of the balance, or Libra, those where the days and nights, being equal, seemed in equilibrium such as that instrument; and stars of the scorpion, those where certain periodical winds bring vapors, burning like the venom of the scorpion.

Men would say by a natural metaphor: The bull spreads over the earth the germs of fecundity (in spring); the ram delivers the skies from the maleficent powers of winter; he saves the world from the serpent (emblem of the humid season) and restores the empire of goodness (summer); the scorpion pours out his poison on the earth and scatters disease and death.

The above is a brief synopsis of the distinguished research scholar Volney in his article on the worship of symbols.

ZODIAC AND ITS MEANING

The word *Zodiac* means an imaginary line or belt in the heavens. It is not a physical body and, obviously, has no gravitational pull. This is why astronomers and astrophysicists are disquieted and perplexed by people who believe in it. Wisely, however, scientists completely reject the so-called influence of the twelve signs, realizing that the astrologers' claim that the influence is due to gravitational attraction is completely absurd.

THE BIBLE AND THE STARS

They fought from heaven; the stars in their courses fought against Sisera (Judges 5:20). Undoubtedly, this means that Sisera realized that his horoscope based on astrological findings was unfavorable. As previously pointed out, this is the psychology of antiquity; and the ancients said that if you were born under a certain sign you would have a certain psychological makeup, such as special traits, characteristics, tendencies, and aptitudes, which would be dominant for you. If Sisera believed that the stars were against him, naturally it would be done unto him as he believed, for the law of life is the law of belief.

All of us are brought up with certain beliefs, opinions, fears, and attitudes toward life. All of us are conditioned differently in our youth. However, there is no fatalism, because we can change our lives by tuning in with the Infinite and claiming that what is true of God is true of us. As we think, speak, and act from the standpoint of the Infinite Presence and Power, so will we cast a spiritual horoscope for ourselves based on wisdom, truth, and Divine law and order.

Obviously, Sisera feared defeat and death. As Job says: *For the thing which I greatly feared is come upon me . . .* (Job 3:25). Such an attitude of mind could only end in disastrous defeat for Sisera. Sisera could have broken and overcome the negative predictions given to him by the astrologer. He could have turned to the God-Presence within and claimed peace, harmony, love, and Divine right action; and his life would have changed. Sisera was a Philistine and was not acquainted with the laws of mind or the way of the Infinite Spirit. His defeat was not in his stars but in his subconscious mind.

The Philistines worshipped idols and stone statues in their temples and looked upon them as gods. Many people calling themselves Christians, Jews, Moslems, and Buddhists fear and give power to the swine flu, germs, the weather, black magic, voodoo, evil spirits, cancer, old age, and death. Yet there is no death— only life; and age is not the flight of years but the dawn of wisdom. A billion years from now you will be alive somewhere, for God is life and God cannot die. His life is your life now.

CALL UPON THIS POWER

No matter who you are or what you are, and regardless of any Zodiacal sign under which you may have been born, you can call upon this Spiritual Presence and Power Which created the universe and Which is Omnipotent, to guide, direct, and heal you. If you open your mind and heart to receive, It will answer you and restore your soul. However, if you believe that Saturn is working against you, then the Infinite cannot work through you.

Rely upon the Spirit within; then all things will become new and all the obstacles and difficulties will melt and dissolve in the same way as the light dispels the darkness.

SORCERY, VOODOO, AND WITCHCRAFT

All these words really mean is the misuse of the Spiritual Power. There is only One Power—God. It is all based on

suggestion. You have the power to reject the ~~creative suggest~~
tions or predictions of others. Think good a~~nd~~
low. Walk in the consciousness of God's love and ra~~
and goodwill to all. You will gradually build up an immun~~
to the negative atmosphere and false beliefs of the world.

Look at voodoo and black magic in their true light. See
them for what they really are; that is to say, they are used by
persons who are ignorant of the real spiritual power. These
people think they know about it, but they don't. When you
see them in their true light, this power falls away. There is
only One Power, and It moves as unity and harmony, and is
the affirmative power. The negative use of the Hidden Power
is destroyed by the constructive use of the Power.

The real and ultimate position is that of conscious union
with the Source of Life. Get acquainted with this and you
need not worry about any action of the negative suggestions
of others. Remember the reciprocity between yourself and
the Infinite Power. The power of suggestion is *a* hidden
power, but the Power Which creates all things is *the* Hidden
Power Which is the Source of all things.

The late Judge Thomas Troward in "The Hidden Power"
states: "If anybody should be, then, so ill-willed towards us
and so lamentably ignorant of spiritual truth himself as to
seek to exercise the power of malicious suggestion against us,
I pity the person who tries to use it. He will get nothing out
of it, because he is firing peas out of a pea-shooter against an
ironclad war vessel. That is what it amounts to; but for himself it amounts to something more." It is a true saying that
"Curses return home to roost."

A GREAT TRUTH

Surely there is no enchantment against Jacob; neither is there any divination against Israel: according to this time it shall be said of Jacob and of Israel, What hath God wrought! (Numbers 23:23). Jacob is man awakening to the Truth of the Divine Presence within him. Israel means a man who believes and knows the sovereignty of the One Spirit and the regnancy of his thought.

But against any of the children of Israel shall not a dog move his tongue . . . (Exodus 11:7).

OUR FIRST CLOCKS

An aerial navigator in Israel said to me that the stars were our first timepiece; and that is right. He shoots the stars on the route he travels and for the time also. The Naval Observatories and the Observatory of Greenwich, England, make use of the stars and the sun to set the clocks to the right time. The stars govern our world to a certain extent, but not in any astrological sense. In the local planetarium the astronomers can take you back thousands of years B.C. because they know the law regarding their movement, which is always mathematically accurate and in perfect precision.

PLANTING AND REAPING

In ancient times men reckoned the time for planting and reaping by the position of the stars. When Aries appeared at a certain place, the Vernal Equinox was near and spring was at hand. The stars are governed by a mathematical precision so rhythmical and godlike that they were worshipped in ancient times. When Libra appeared at a certain spot in the celestial atmosphere, it was the Autumnal Equinox and autumn was near. It was the time of the harvest, and the deciduous trees shed their leaves.

CYCLES OF LIFE

There are the cycles of childhood, adolescence, youth, manhood, and old age; and there are yearly cycles, daily cycles, weekly and monthly cycles, and hourly cycles. The cycles of your mental life are based upon your ideas, beliefs, opinions, and convictions which revolve in your consciousness and which come forth according to their nature.

The sun in the heavens was a symbol of God to the ancients. They looked upon its functions as Godlike in relation to the earth. They knew the sun was not God, but it reminded them of the real Invisible Light within. The stars of God represent the stars of truth within you. They symbolize the knowledge, the awareness, the wisdom, and the creative ideas which light up the heavens of your mind, giving you peace, harmony, joy, abundance, and security.

It is foolish, therefore, to worship the stars or the planets, which are only masses of molecular combinations moving in space. Instead, why not worship and give all of your allegiance to the Infinite Intelligence in which you live, move, and have your being.

4

What Is Truth?

AT NEW DELHI we explored both New and Old Delhi, visiting Gandhi's Tomb and Jama Mosque, the Red Fort, Moonlight Square, and many other fascinating and interesting places of historical and religious interest. Jaipur and the famous City Palace, which now houses a museum containing rare manuscripts, is well worth visiting.

We had the rare opportunity of visiting the Taj Mahal during the full moon at night. All of those in our group remained silent for about twenty minutes, contemplating its rare beauty, symmetry, order, and proportion. It is called one of the Seven Wonders of the World and was built by Emperor Shahjehan as a mausoleum for his Queen Mumtaz Mahal in white marble. It is a universal symbol of love. Its walls and palaces, famous for their intricate inlay work, are silent witnesses to the mathematical and geometric skill of the ancient Indian builders. Undoubtedly, they belonged to

ancient guilds composed of men initiated into the act of por-
traying beauty, love, and Divine order in stone and marble
edifices. The Taj Mahal may be called a "love story in stone."

Our visit to Banares was very instructive and rewarding.
Our guide gave a very fine dissertation on the religious customs, burial procedures, and history of the many famous
temples and mosques of both the Buddhists and the Hindus.
The idea for this chapter came to me when a member of our
group asked the guide: "Do you think the Buddhists' beliefs
represent the Truth?" He responded: "What is Truth?" Two
plus two equal four. Buddha taught the Truth when he said
"ignorance is the only sin." I thought that the young man had
replied quite intelligently.

You will recall the following from the Book of John: *Pilate
saith unto him, What is truth? And when he had said this, he went
out again unto the Jews, and saith unto them, I find in him no fault
at all* (John 18:38). You will notice that Pilate's question was
not answered. Truth is God and God is Truth, and God cannot be known in the absolute sense. However, we can learn the
laws of our mind and begin to think right, feel right, and act
right, thus transforming our lives. The ancients said: "Truth is
learned in the silence, truth is felt in silence, truth is transmit-
ted in the silence; for God abides in the silence."

One woman in our group said that Christianity was the
Truth; others thought Buddhism was the Truth, and one of
our Hindu friends believed that the Gita contained all the
Truth. If a man says Catholicism is the Truth, he is immediately challenged by a Baptist or some other denomination.

Suppose you have people claiming to be Christian Scientists, Unitarians, Divine Scientists, Religious Scientists, Catholics, Protestants, Buddhists, etc., all claiming to have the Truth. It would be somewhat similar to the fable of the blind men describing an elephant. There is only one Truth, one Law, one Life, one Power, one Substance, one God—the Father of all—the Life Principle—from which all things come. This is why Jesus was silent when he was asked the question. Truth is the Silent Presence, the I AM, or God, in all of us. The Bible says: . . . *I am the way, the truth, and the life* . . . (John 14:6). I AM means Being, Life, Awareness, God—the Self-Originating Spirit within you, without face, form, and figure.

If you claim that Buddhism is the Truth, you may have an argument on your hands. Whenever you put a label on It, you don't have the Truth. The old saying which is lost in the mists of time is very appropriate: "When you name It, you cannot find It, and when you find It, you cannot name It." It is the Nameless One within you, without face, form, or figure, timeless, shapeless, and ageless. How could you put a label on It?

For example, how could you label love, peace, harmony, joy, goodwill, inspiration, guidance, beauty, laughter, honesty, integrity, or justice? Surely you would not refer to these qualities and attributes as Catholic, Protestant, Jewish, or Hindu. Neither would you label the principles of chemistry, physics, astronomy, mathematics, etc. All these are cosmic and universal and are available to all men. God is no respecter of persons.

. . . *I perceive that God is no respecter of persons* (Acts 10:34).

YOU ARE IN A WORLD OF OPPOSITES

If it is raining and very foggy and you are going on a journey, you might say, "It's a bad day today." The farmer whose land is suffering from drought says, "It's a wonderful day," and he blesses and rejoices in the rain. The facts of life are not the same to all people. Anything you say about religion or politics has its opposite and an opposing argument.

Emerson in "Compensation" elaborates on this subject, which he calls: "Polarity, or action and reaction, we meet in every part of nature; in darkness and light; in heat and cold; in the ebb and flow of waters; in male and female; in the inspiration and expiration of plants and animals; in the systole and diastole of the heart; in the undulation of fluids and of sound; in the centrifugal and centripetal gravity; in electricity, galvanism, and chemical affinity. Superinduce magnetism at one end of the needle; the opposite magnetism takes place at the other end. If the south attracts, the north repels. To empty here, you must condense there. An inevitable dualism bisects nature, so that each thing is a half and suggests another thing to make it whole, as spirit, matter; man, woman; odd, even; subjective, objective; in, out; upper, lower; motion, rest; yea, nay."

The late Judge Thomas Troward, author of many books on mental science, said that if a thing is true, there is a way in which it is true. For example, a man may say: "Strawberries gives me hives," yet millions of people eat strawberries and do not get hives; rather, they look upon the berries as a universal food item. The man who is allergic to strawberries has made a law unto himself so that what he says is true for him. But it is not a cosmic or universal truth. If it were, everybody who eats strawberries would suffer from the same disturbance. Each of these two opposite statements is true in its own way. He manifests his personal relationship to strawberries.

YOU CAN BE CHANGED

One of the men on our trip said to me that human nature can't be changed. Then he elaborated on the crime and savagery going on in different parts of the world and the brutalities and torture practiced on all sides in the recent wars. I pointed out to him that he can't make dogmatic and authoritative statements like that without being challenged. Every priest, rabbi, minister, psychologist, psychiatrist, and medical doctor has seen miraculous changes take place within an individual. The author has witnessed the complete transformation of murderers, alcoholics, and dope fiends who subsequently became great boons and blessings to humanity.

Generally speaking, we may note that human nature has not changed much in the last 2,000 or 3,000 years; but look at the many thousands of people down through the ages who have completely changed and have decided to lead God-like lives. If you are an attorney pleading a case for your client, you will admit that the opposing counsel can build up an excellent case for his side. His contradictions of all your points seem just as logical as yours. Likewise, the Buddhist can build up an excellent case on his side, just as the Christian theologian can build up a good case for his beliefs.

The Truth Always Works

. . . Do men gather grapes of thorns, or figs of thistles? (Matthew 7:16). *Wherefore by their fruits ye shall know them* (Matthew 7:20).

Truth is one and indivisible, for God is Truth—the same yesterday, today, and forever. Many people are perplexed and bewildered by the complexities of conflicting theologies, and they hunger and thirst for the Truth which will set them free. For example, the various denominations in Christianity as well as other religious groups disagree among themselves in their creedal assumptions and practices. Moreover, the teaching of the hundreds of sects, not only in Christianity but in other religions of the world, is full of inconsistencies and absurdities.

Truth sets you free from fear, ignorance, superstition, sickness, lack, and limitation; it solves your problems and brings peace to the troubled mind. You will meet people in many parts of the world who have no religious affiliation of any kind; but they are full of faith and confidence in the goodness of God, and in the guidance and love of God. They have an inner peace and an inner light; they are prosperous and full of goodwill and the laughter of God.

Religion is of the heart; not of the lips. They bring forth the fruits of the Spirit, which is the real test for Truth. Truth always heals. When you are happy, joyous, free, and expressing vitality, peace, and abundance, you are revealing the fruits of the Spirit. There is no such thing as undemonstrated Truth: As within, so without; as without, so within. There can be nothing in your subconscious mind that is not made manifest sooner or later in the outer phases of your life.

THE LAW OF LIFE

. . . *If thou canst believe, all things are possible to him that believeth* (Mark 9:23). What do you believe about Life, God, the Universe? The answer you give to that question determines everything in your outer world. You are belief expressed. Learn to believe in the creative laws of your mind. Know that your thoughts are creative. What you imagine and feel you experience. Cease believing in creeds, sectarian concepts, liturgies, ceremonies, and rituals.

Believe that the Infinite Intelligence responds when you call upon It. Believe in a God of love governing you, guiding you, watching over you, and you will prosper beyond your fondest dreams. You don't have to believe in Catholicism, Buddhism, Judaism, Shintoism, or Hinduism. You don't have to believe in any rites, wafers, wines, statues, men, or saints.

WHERE IS YOUR FAITH?

The Bible says: . . . *According to your faith be it unto you* (Matthew 9:29). In response to the question: "What is your faith?," some will say, "I'm a Mormon," "Jew," "Protestant," "Buddhist," etc. Faith is an attitude of mind—a way of thinking. It is an awareness of the Indwelling God and of your capacity to let it function in all phases of your life.

You have faith when you know that whatever is impressed on the subconscious will be expressed. Faith has nothing to do with creeds, dogmas, or traditional rites, formulations, ceremonies, or doctrinal beliefs expressed by churches. Your faith is what you really believe deep down in your heart—your real inner conviction about God and life in general.

What are your emotional espousals and inner beliefs about yourself and your inner powers? Your subconscious assumptions, beliefs, and convictions dictate and control all your conscious actions. The Bible states what real religion is all about: *For as he thinketh in his heart* (subconscious mind), *so is he* . . . (Proverbs 23:7).

ONE FUNDAMENTAL TRUTH

Underneath all the religions of the world, realize there is but One God and One Truth. All the doctrines, teachings, and rituals deal with the relativity of Truth. A man may say to you: "I offered incense and a lighted candle and certain prayers at the shrine of Buddha and I received a miraculous healing in response to my prayer." His prayer was answered, not because of the candle, incense, or shrine, but because of his subconscious belief. In other words, he answered his own prayer. His subconscious responded to his blind belief. That is the truth about it; not the reason which he gave. According to his belief was it done unto him.

CHANGE ETERNAL IS AT THE ROOT OF ALL THINGS

Everything changes. Every time you get a new idea or a new concept of Truth, you have changed physiologically. You are constantly changing. You have a new physical body every eleven months. Constant change is at the root of all things.

The late Ernest Holmes, author of *Science of Mind*, once told me that three men on his block made a dogmatic statement and reached the positive conclusion that a certain man they saw going down the street in the direction of a cocktail lounge was going to that bar to get drunk. He asked them why they were so certain and definite in their statement. They answered that every day at the same time in the evening this man appeared and went directly to the bar. However, this particular evening he went to the door of the tavern and turned back and never went there again. He had suddenly decided to stop drinking and to become a new man.

This indicates that you can't come to an absolute judgment about anything in the world. They forgot the great Truth: . . . *Be ye transformed by the renewing of your mind* . . . (Romans 12:2).

Looking at the Two Sides

A woman may come to see you and tell you all the reasons why she wants a divorce. What she says may sound plausible and logical. A few hours later, her husband, not knowing that his wife had come to see you, may visit you and tell you all the reasons why he wants to preserve the marriage. He may also sound logical and reasonable in his conclusions. Both of them cannot be right, but each one is looking at the situation from his or her individual viewpoint.

Many times these couples seeking a divorce will tell you that a marriage counselor had told them that they had to adjust to reality, and they are confused by the word *reality*, which is relative and based on the person's attitude towards life in general. There is Divine Reality, for example, which refers to the Changeless Being called God, Which never changes. But the world in which we live is constantly changing its standards, mores, and mode of living.

What both the husband and wife mentioned above really want is peace, harmony, love, understanding, and goodwill. If each of them will sincerely pray for these qualities, they will either be drawn closer together or find their highest happiness apart. Infinite Intelligence will solve the problem for them.

There are two sides to the divorce question, just as there are two opposing viewpoints to every proposition, whether political, religious, concerning human relations, or whatnot. There are two ends of the stick and an inside and outside to yourself and everything else in the universe.

Einstein stated the whole matter succinctly when he said: "The world we see is the world we are." In other words, your inner world represents your habitual thinking, beliefs, opinions, imagery, training, and indoctrination. You are always projecting your inner state of mind onto people, conditions, and events. You look at people and conditions through the content of your mental imagery. If you look through the eyes of love and understanding, you will see a different world and you will also react differently to people and circumstances.

There are two realities: the external world to which you react and the inner world of thought, feeling, and imagery. The secret is to reconcile the opposites and experience peace and equanimity. The man or woman who looks out through the eyes of hatred and resentment colors everything he sees and hears with that attitude of mind, and his relationships with people and events generally result in chaos, suffering, and misery. If, for example, you pour a teaspoonful of black ink or some indigo dye into a gallon of distilled water, you color the entire contents.

Your consciousness determines your relationship with the external world and with other people. Your state of consciousness is the way you think, feel, believe, and whatever you consent to mentally. This attitude of mind is definitely and positively the cause of all your experiences in life. Your associates and acquaintances react differently to life's experiences based on their attitudes, beliefs, and inner emotional espousals.

The following ancient saying sums it all up: "What thou seest, man, that too become thou must, God if thou seest God and dust if thou seest dust."

HE WAS ALLERGIC TO HAM

I remember the case of a soldier in the First World War who had told the sergeant, "I can't eat ham. I break out in a terrible rash." The sergeant said there was nothing in the regulations that says you must eat ham, and then walked away. After a long, twenty-mile hike through rough country, a concoction was served by the sergeant, of which the particular soldier ate generously. The following day the sergeant told the soldier that ham was the major ingredient of the concoction served and that he had not broken out in a rash. Everybody laughed, including the soldier.

He was healed of a false belief. The soldier did not know he had been eating ham, inasmuch as the mess sergeant had disguised it by mixing it with many other ingredients; therefore, the soldier, not knowing that it contained ham, had no reaction. It seems that this particular soldier, as a child, had eaten some ham, which apparently was tainted, and he had become ill. His mother had told him he must never touch it again.

You can readily see that it was thus a subconscious fear or belief on his part. There was nothing bad for his health in the ham served by the army. The soldier had had a very poor personal relationship to ham and was now healed by laughing it off.

PROPAGANDA AND ITS EFFECT

Many people ask me whether they should smoke or not and what I think about the cancer scare due to cigarettes. My answer is that each must follow his own belief about smoking. It is a personal decision; therefore, if a person is afraid that cigarettes or smoking a pipe could bring on cancer, he should avoid them. It is done to each according to his belief. I know people here in Leisure World and have known many in Beverly Hills who are advanced in years (eighty to ninety), who have smoked cigarettes for fifty to sixty years and who have had no bad reaction at all. This is true all over the world.

The effect of cigarettes upon different people is entirely different, based on their mental makeup. Medical men know that thousands of people who smoke cigarettes get lung cancer; again, thousands of people who smoke cigarettes constantly do not get lung cancer. So it is foolish to make authoritative and absolute pronouncements, such as "If you smoke you will get cancer." It depends upon the particular person.

Job said: *For the thing which I greatly feared is come upon me . . .* (Job 3:25). There is a mass mind belief regarding the effects of nicotine in cigarettes and tobacco, and this mass mind impinges on all of us. But if we rise above the mass mind, we can then neutralize the effect. I am now thinking of a relative who smoked constantly, teaching past ninety-nine years of age. He never suffered any ill effects from smoking. He never heard of cigarette cancer scares and the dire effects of smoking given out by the medical profession and by the news media today. Obviously, he had no fear of ill effects. In his own way he believed that smoking was relaxing and soothing, and he enjoyed it. I am sure it was done unto him according to his belief.

What is your personal belief? Follow your belief, as it is the principal factor in all this propaganda.

THE ONE GREAT CERTAINTY

The one great Truth is that God is God and the Law is Law— the same yesterday, today, and forever. The Truth is constant and invariable. God is timeless, changeless, ageless, absolute harmony, the eternal now!

A woman here in Leisure World, Laguna Hills, told me that she had been absolutely sure that her father in Chicago would give her $10,000 to pay off the mortgage which was pressing upon her. On the phone he had said that he would mail her a certified cashier's check and she was elated, but before he could send it, he died of a sudden heart attack.

You cannot be absolutely sure about anything in this changing world but one thing: God is God and never changes. You can absolutely trust the Infinite Presence and Power. It is always the same—yesterday, today, and forever—absolute, beyond time and space, and beyond all argument, disputation, and dialectics. Place your trust and confidence in the Infinite, which lies stretched in smiling repose.

HE WAS A CONSTANT LOSER

I had a most interesting conversation with another man during this trip around the world. As a young man, he said, he had played the horses and had lost constantly. He squandered about $2,500 in gambling at the race track, believing that he had acquired a system. When he lost, he tried to get his money back by betting larger and larger sums of money. Of course, due to his fear, however, he continued to lose.

One day he went to the track with his last $2 to place on a sure thing. He lost. He was now penniless. Suddenly he found a $100 bill on the grass and was naturally elated, telling himself that his luck had changed and that he was going to recoup his losses. He had a new frame of mind and had supreme confidence in his good fortune. He picked five winners, which paid him large sums of money. The next day, though, he was visited by Secret Service men advising him that the $100 bill was a counterfeit. He had been identified by the cashier.

His explanation satisfied them, but he then realized for the first time in his life that it was his confidence and faith that had produced the results; not the worthless piece of paper. This was the turning point in his life. From that moment forward, he forgot about trying to make a fortune by depending on horses; rather, he placed his confidence on the Eternal Source, Which never fails and which is absolutely dependable and absolutely trustworthy; and because of that One Great Truth and certainty, he is now travelling and lecturing around the world. He has found peace, joy, and strength in this changing world.

But they that wait upon the Lord shall renew their strength; they shall mount up with wings as eagles; they shall run, and not be weary; and they shall walk, and not faint (Isaiah 40:31).

5

The True Art of Meditation and Relaxation

KATMANDU, THE CAPITAL of the Himalayan Kingdom of Nepal, the "Shangri La" of the travel world, is located on the southern slopes of the mighty Himalayas between India and Tibet. This is a country that has been isolated for centuries by its rulers. Nepal has wonderful, unique sights to offer travellers from all over the world.

Nepal is famous for its scenic beauty and the glorious, panoramic view of the snowy ranges. The town of Patan is lined with pagodas, the Krishna Temple, and the Golden Temple, which is outstanding in beauty. Here we saw a number of elderly men meditating on the temple steps and at the entrances to the various shrines. Their eyes were closed and some seemed to be in a mystic trance. The idea for a chapter on meditation and relaxation came to my mind.

How to Meditate Constructively and Easily

There is no mystery about meditation. Everybody in the world meditates, but not always constructively. Meditation is as natural as eating, drinking, breathing, etc. The businessman, the scientist, the housewife, and the taxi driver all meditate. Even the agnostic, the atheist, and the most seemingly materialistic minded business people constantly meditate. The only difference is that they do not meditate on spiritual things—on the eternal verities, which are the same yesterday, today, and forever. When you meditate from a spiritual standpoint, it is absolutely essential to practice the Presence of God.

True Spiritual Meditation

True meditation is a way of experiencing the Presence of God. It is the quickest method of becoming illumined, inspired, and absorbed in the Truths of God and of experiencing the moment that lasts forever. This simply means that you become engrossed in God, knowing, believing, and intensely confirming that the Living Spirit Almighty within you is the only Presence, Power, Cause, and Substance, and that everything you are aware of is a part of the Infinite Being in manifestation. Sit down quietly, relax your mind, and focus your attention on this greatest of all truths; then you are truly meditating from a spiritual standpoint because you are mentally ingesting, digesting, absorbing, and appropriating this truth into your mentality in the same manner as that in which an apple becomes a part of your blood stream.

Everybody Meditates Either Constructively or Negatively

For example, John Jones gets up in the morning and immediately picks up the newspaper, reading the headlines dealing with politics, crime, and international disturbances. Many times he gets agitated and disturbed about the political situation. He gets furious at the decisions of some judges and terribly exercised about what certain columnists had written. He is so absorbed and engrossed in his mental recriminations that when his wife speaks to him, he does not hear her.

This is a first-class meditation having very negative results. Know that whatever we get absorbed in or give our attention to is magnified by our subconscious. The newspaper has no power to disturb him, as the written material, which is printed in ink, has no power to irritate him or give him indigestion. It was all due to the movement of his own thoughts. He disturbed himself. He could have read the newspaper dispassionately. He might be moved at times to write constructive letters to his congressman or to the appropriate governing bodies in his city, but the newspaper and its contents had absolutely no power whatever to annoy him.

People all over the world meditate on old hurts, peeves, grudges, grievances, lawsuits they lost, a blowout on a lonely road, losses they suffered in the 1929 stock market crash, and the mistakes they have made, not knowing that they are simply magnifying the troubles and reinfecting themselves all over again. If a negative thought comes into your mind, cremate it with a spiritual thought such as, "God is love, and His peace fills my soul."

For example, if you are dwelling on what the prophets of doom and gloom today are predicting, or if you are mentally quarreling with the boss on the job, you are indulging in a first-rate meditation, which is followed by negative results. Ouspensky used to say that one's inner speech becomes solidified sound, which means that your silent conversation with yourself is always made manifest in your experience. The silent thinking and imaging, whether constructive or negative, comes forth as form, function, experience, and event in your life.

THE FRUITS OF HER SPIRITUAL MEDITATION

I received a lovely letter from a woman in Oregon who had a malignant tumor. She had been reading *Great Bible Truths for Human Problems** and had become intensely interested in the techniques of prayer outlined therein. She had begun to meditate on the God-Presence, reminding herself that the Infinite Healing Presence was within her and that God was boundless love, absolute harmony, infinite intelligence, omnipotent, all-wise, and omnipresent. She then claimed for about fifteen or twenty minutes two or three times a day that "God is, and His Healing Presence is now flowing through me. Divine love saturates my whole being and God in the midst of me is making me whole and perfect now. I give thanks for the miraculous healing taking place now. It is done!"

In about a week's time she knew that something had happened, and her surgeon confirmed her intuitive perception.

---

* *Great Bible Truths for Human Problems* by Dr. Joseph Murphy, DeVorss & Co., Inc., Marina del Rey, California, 1976.

The tumor was dissolved, and X-rays showed nothing there. This is spiritual meditation. It produced results. You are living in a subjective and objective world, and you must show results in both phases of your life.

WHAT IS MEDITATION?

The Bible is replete with references to meditation. To meditate, in the language of the dictionary, means to keep the mind or attention focused upon; to muse upon or over; to consider something to be done or affected; to engage in thought or contemplation; to ruminate, reflect, cogitate, study, think. That is why everybody meditates.

WHAT DOES THE BIBLE SAY?

The Psalmist says: *But his delight is in the law of the Lord; and in his law doth he meditate day and night. And he shall be like a tree planted by the rivers of water, that bringeth forth his fruit in his season; his leaf also shall not wither; and whatsoever he doeth shall prosper* (Psalm 1:2–3).

Let the words of my mouth, and the meditation of my heart, be acceptable in thy sight, O Lord, my strength, and my redeemer (Psalm 19:14).

As the Psalmist points out, your delight is in the law of the Lord, and the law is: You are what you contemplate. You are what you think all day long. Give your attention and devotion to the great truth: . . . *As he thinketh in his heart, so is he* (Proverbs 23:7).

It is the ideas, beliefs, and opinions impressed in your sub-conscious mind that are projected and made manifest on the screen of space. You must incorporate the eternal truths of God in your subjective depths before they will become oper-ative in your life. You must, therefore, practice contemplating on the great truths of God from the highest standpoint.

Follow the injunction of the Psalmist when he says: *Let the words* (thoughts expressed) *of my mouth, and the meditation of my heart* (the inner, silent knowing of the soul; your deep, abiding faith and conviction) *be acceptable . . .* (Psalm 19:14).

In other words, in true spiritual meditation, your brain and your heart must agree on what you affirm. To state it still another way, your conscious and subconscious mind must both agree; then comes the manifestation of your good. Your thought and feeling, fused together, represent the union of the male and female elements within you, which are Divine agencies, resulting in the joy of the answered prayer.

The Moment that Lasts Forever

In talking about meditation during my visit to India, a man who had been a chronic alcoholic and a dope addict (he had used cocaine from time to time and told me he had even hit the gutter and had become a panhandler) related that one day he had met a holy man. (There are about two million roaming the country in India.) The holy man told him that all he had to do was to still the wheels of his mind and for about half an hour, twice a day, affirm: "Brahma's love, peace, beauty, glory, and light are flowing through my whole being, purifying, cleansing, healing, and restoring my soul."

He followed the instructions, knowing that he would activate and resurrect the qualities and powers of God resident in his subjective depths. He continued meditating every night and morning; and at the end of a few weeks, while meditating one night, his whole mind and body, as well as the room he was in, became a blaze of light. He was actually blinded, as was Paul, by the light for awhile. He felt an inner rapture and ecstasy and a sense of oneness with God and the whole world. His feeling was indescribable.

He had experienced what the ancient mystics called "the moment that lasts forever." He was completely healed and is teaching others how to lead a new life. He invested his mind wisely—that is real meditation.

MEDITATION MOLDS YOUR FUTURE

You are what you meditate on all day long. The late Dr. David Seabury, who specialized in Quimby's techniques, told me that while he was practicing in New York City, a man had asked him to come and see his wife, who was paralyzed due to an emotional shock. Dr. Seabury called it psychological paralysis. He gave her a technique to practice. She was to vividly imagine herself doing all the things she would do were she whole and perfect, such as driving her car, riding horseback, golfing, and working around the house.

She practiced this for about fifteen or twenty minutes four

or five times a day, regularly and systematically. He explained to her that any image she held in her mind, backed by faith and enthusiasm, would come to pass and be objectified. At the end of a month, he arranged with the nurses to absent themselves temporarily at a time arranged by him, simultaneously informing the woman that her son would call from India at that hour. (All this had been arranged with the son beforehand.)

At exactly 12:00 noon, the phone rang and kept on ringing, she knowing it was her son. The phone had been purposely placed out of her reach. She got up and walked to the phone and has continued walking for many years afterwards.

She had been very busy for a month focussing her attention on walking, riding, etc. She had expended a vast amount of mental and spiritual energy towards a specific goal of walking again. Her mental image was energized by faith and confidence in the Power within her. She had been truly meditating. Then, when she heard the phone ring, knowing her son was to call at that hour, the longing to hear his voice seized her mind and activated the Spirit within and she experienced the results of her meditation. Her thought-image was the mediator between the invisible world of Spirit (God) and its physical manifestation of walking.

TRANSCENDENTAL MEDITATION

Emerson was a transcendentalist, and he healed himself of tuberculosis by meditating on the beauties and glories of nature. He wrote a magnificent chapter on nature, saying: "Crossing a bare common, in snow puddles, at twilight, under a clouded sky, without having in my thoughts any thoughts of special good fortune, I have enjoyed a perfect exhilaration. The currents of the Universal Being circulate through me; I am part and parcel of God."

In meditating and writing on the beauty, order, symmetry, and proportion evident in all nature and contemplating the glories of the stars and the celestial beauty, he brought about a molecular change in his body to conform to the pattern on the Mount. He called the stars the daily bread of the soul. His contemplation transcended his five senses, and he dwelt on the One, the Beautiful, and the Good in himself and in all of nature. He practiced real transcendental meditation.

The Om Mantra

In the East, the word "Om," which in our Bible is called I AM, means Being, Life, God, Awareness, the Living Spirit Almighty. Many repeat the word "Om" over and over again as a chant. You can repeat "I AM" to yourself over and over again; and as you continue, you will find an inner peace and tranquility.

A mantra can be a verse from the Bible, a word, a hymn, or the sound "Om" repeated over and over again. "The Lord is my shepherd" is a good mantra. It is much better to know the meaning of what you are affirming than to use a mantra blindly without knowing what you are saying. Your repetitions will get no real result without meaning. If you want to grow spiritually you should know what you are doing and why. There must be meaning and feeling behind the verse, mantra, or word.

You can use the word "peace," repeating it for fifteen or twenty minutes, and you will become very peaceful, relaxed, serene, and calm. Another wonderful mantra is "God is love." A businessman told me that at the suggestion of a professor of psychology, he took the word "Coca Cola" and repeated it to himself for twenty minutes twice a day. He said his blood pressure dropped, his digestion improved, and he felt relaxed and more peaceful. The psychologist had wanted to point out to him that any word used over and over again would bring relaxation of mind and body, resulting in better circulation, digestion, and the release of more energy.

He produced a quiet mind by focussing on one word. Likewise, you can take any word, such as "insight," and repeat it and get the same results. The one word, "Coca Cola," may well bring about the bodily changes mentioned; but that is not really spiritual growth, because to meditate spiritually, you must appropriate more and more of Divinity and become a more God-like man.

CLEANSE YOUR MIND

Before you meditate spiritually, forgive yourself completely for any negative thoughts and resolve not to harbor them again. Furthermore, forgive everybody else by radiating love and goodwill to them while wishing for them all the blessings of life. You will always know when you have forgiven everyone, because you can meet them in your mind and you no longer sizzle; you are at peace. You would not pour clean water into a dirty vessel. The vessel is your mind. You don't expect the Holy Spirit to flow through a contaminated mind. Resentment, self-condemnation, hostility, and ill will block the flow of good into your life. Meditate the right way. *And when ye stand praying, forgive, if ye have ought against any . . .* (Mark 11:25).

The Effortless Way

The discipline of looking inwardly is meditation. What we understand we do naturally; what we do not understand we force ourselves to do. Students so often tell the teacher how hard they have tried. The very effort meant failure, for meditation is always effortless. Tension, exertion, and force are fatal and will only result in failure.

An excellent way, for example, to still the mind is as follows: Imagine yourself on a mountaintop, looking into a lake. In the placid surface you see the sky, the stars, the moon, and those things above the earth. If the surface of the lake is disturbed, the things seen are blurred and indistinct. Thus, it is with you, if you are not "still"—not at peace.

And the answer to prayer comes only to the man who dwells with all tranquility on the joy of already having received that for which he prayed. Meditation may be called the internalizing of consciousness; it is the pilgrimage within to the Divine Presence.

Half an hour a day spent on meditation upon your ideals, goals, and ambitions will make you a different person. In a few months' time the gentle, silent acknowledgment comes that God is within you; that the Spirit of the Almighty is now moving on your behalf and that which you long to be, to possess, and to do is already a fact of mental acceptance.

Man actualizes this state by feeling the thrill of accomplishment; and when he has succeeded, he will no longer be worried, anxious, or apprehensive. Moreover, he will not ask anyone for advice, because he will be under compulsion to do that which is right. His subjective mind compels him to take all the necessary steps for the completion of his goal or objective.

After prayer, if a man is still doubtful and he begins to argue with himself as to which course to pursue, it means that he has not fixed the desired state in his subconscious. *For I say unto you, Among those that are born of women there is not a greater prophet than John the Baptist: but he that is least in the kingdom of God is greater than he* (Luke 7:28). This means that any man who prays successfully and who touches Reality by getting into the proper mood or feeling is greater than the wisest man alive.

Most of us live life looking outwardly. The wise learn to look inwardly. The disciplines of looking inwardly are termed together "meditation." Detachment is the key to meditation; that is, severing ourselves completely from all worldly beliefs and opinions, focussing silently on our ideal state. It is the effortless-effort which causes us to flow towards that which we realize without conflict. Detachment does not mean that we give up our earthly possessions, which are necessary for our survival; but, rather, we must give up possessiveness in ourselves by realizing that God possesses all and that we are

stewards of the Divine, handling what we possess wisely, judiciously, and constructively. We must not give up what we
have, but rather give up the attachment that peculiarly limits
us to a human viewpoint in all matters.

Be Still and Know I Am God (Psalm 46:10)

Quiet your mind and remind yourself that the "I AM" within
you is God, the only Presence and Power. Stillness is not only
keeping quiet; it means that the causes within the mind by
which the inward life is rendered discordant have been removed. It means that there must be no inner dissonance; but,
rather, that when man goes within himself, he must find perfect and abiding peace.

Knowing that God is within himself makes man live in a
world that is ever peaceful. The lack of it makes man live in a
series of conditions which grieve him to the end. He fusses
and fumes about things which, if he saw them differently,
would not cause one moment of unhappiness.

Every day of our lives we should meditate on beauty, love, and
peace. We should feel that these qualities are being resurrected in
us. As we meditate on wisdom, truth, and beauty, we will experience the second birth, or spiritual awakening.

Moving Inward

By moving inward and meditating on the I AM, or God, the
mystic finally finds the Real. As he goes inward, he realizes
first that this thing called the body is simply waves of light,

and that this earth upon which we are seated becomes flames of light. The external life becomes the dream, and the internal life awakens. As man moves further and further inward, he finally merges with the Infinite. Suddenly man, the meditator, perceives that by going inward he has found the universe; that the sun, moon, stars, and planets are within. For the first time he knows that planets are thoughts; that suns and moons are thoughts; that his own consciousness or I AMness is the realization which sustains them all; that temporarily in space are moving the dreams of the dreamer; and the worlds, suns, moons, and stars are thoughts of the Thinker. God is meditating, and we are His meditation. It is God meditating on the mysteries of Himself.

This inward journey, therefore, ultimately leads man to Nirvana—to the Real; it leads man away from the sense of the small "I" to the realization of the Indwelling God—the Eternal Self. The mystic's mind, through meditation, finds the peace, the strength, and the fortitude for further steps. The practice of the discipline of meditation bestows beauty, love, peace, grace, and dignity upon every impulse, every attitude, and every act.

Let us meditate on these lines, written by the finger of God, the Ancient of Days, which have come to us down through the ages, ever the Ageless Wisdom: "Of all existence I AM the Source, the continuation and the end. I AM the germ, I AM the growth, I AM the decay. All things and creatures I send forth. I support them while they yet stand without, and when the dream of separation ends, I cause their return unto myself.

I AM the Life, the Wheel of the Law, and the way that leadeth to the beyond. There is none else."

RELAXATION

The following is a very old technique of relaxation practiced
in India, Nepal, and other countries:

1. Your chest, neck, and head should be held in as straight
   a line as possible.
2. Then inhale through the nostrils, mentally counting six
   pulse-throbs.
3. Hold your breath during three counts.
4. Exhale through the nostrils six counts.
5. Hold the lungs empty during three counts.
6. Repeat as often as desired, as no slightest discomfort
   is felt.

After a little practice, the rhythm will be perfectly established without the necessity of mental counting. When this is
achieved, all tenseness and effort will disappear and complete
relaxation results.

Later you can execute this exercise with perfect ease while
walking, making each step a rhythmic unit of count. However, in the beginning, especially for people living in the city
where they experience constant interruption of traffic cross-
ings and congestion, it is better to confine the exercise to the
sitting or lying down posture.

In addition to the physical reaction of this rhythmic breathing, there is a spiritual response. With each inhalation, you may impregnate your subconscious with whatever idea you wish. It is important to remember that the suggestion or idea you have in mind should be practiced simultaneously with the inbreathing. In this relaxed state, there is an outcropping of the subconscious, which is the best and easiest way to impregnate your deeper mind. For example, if you are gloomy or despondent, as you inbreathe, orally or mentally say, "I AM happy" and feel it. Smile. This exercise may be repeated twenty-four to a hundred times at one time and repeated as often as you like.

LEARNING TO BREATHE RHYTHMICALLY

When we learn to breathe rhythmically, its effect on the nervous system is such that all tension is dissolved. All of us know from a physiological standpoint, deep, diaphragmatic breathing is very beneficial in promoting bodily well-being. The sensation of wellbeing, which always follows the drawing of a deep breath, favors the acceptance of any new idea or suggestion.

During these breathing exercises, we should visualize ourselves as we long to be—full of vigor and health. The regular rhythm of breathing brings about a stimulus analogous to that exerted by every rhythm, such as, for example, music or dance forms which have a soothing, lulling influence. This rhythm tends to immobilize the attention and induce relaxation.

HEALED OF ASTHMA

In talking to an elderly woman in the hotel at Katmandu, Nepal, she said that she had suffered from asthma for several years and that a priest in one of the temples had given her a spiritual formula which had healed her of the affliction. The spiritual exercise was as follows:

She sat down quietly in her arm chair and began to breathe slowly. With each inhalation she would silently affirm, "I AM all health." With each exhalation she would affirm, "God is my health." She would keep this up for from ten to fifteen minutes, morning and evening and also at noon.

In two weeks' time she was healed and is now vital, strong, and bubbling over with enthusiasm at the young age of eighty years.

YOUR BODY IS CONSTANTLY CHANGING

Man is a pulsating, rhythmic being. Our bodies are as much subject to rhythmic laws as is everything else in the universe. The ancients said, "Every atom in space dances to the rhythm of the gods." The universe (one verse) is simply one note or tone in God; but there is an infinite number of tones or rates of vibration within the one. Everything that we see is vibrating, and nothing is in absolute rest in nature. Only God is motionless. Nature is the birth or activity of God—the One manifesting Himself in countless ways. The moment forms appear in the world, they begin to change; and from them appear other forms, and so on ad infinitum.

Forms are simply appearances; they come and go. Likewise, the body of man is constantly changing. Science tells us that man has a new body every eleven months. The cells of the body are constantly dying, being replaced by new cells. If man spiritualizes his thoughts, the cells of the body will take on a new spiritual overtone, and his whole being will be transformed into vitality and wholeness.

There is almost a complete change in the chemistry of the body in a matter of seconds and minutes, so much so that scarcely one atom or electron composing your body will be present a few months hence. All is vibration, and constant change pervades the universe. The beating of your heart follows a certain rhythm; so also does the ebb and flow of the tide.

Cease Blaming Others

We must realize that the cause underlying most failures to effectual prayer is muddled thinking and lack of emotional control. The important thing to observe is that we find the same law operating in the magnetic attraction of impulses of fear, jealousy, anger, and despair (which are responsible for most of the failures and frustrations in life) as we find in the ineffable emotion of love, which results in good. A single principle, an identical force, lies underneath accomplishment or failure.

Fear begets inescapable trouble and tribulation. Manifestations and experiences differ according to the emotional attitude and mood of the individual. It might well be said that all disease has its origin in emotional frustration. Man is the product of his emotions and moods.

The tendency in many people is to project blame onto others for the unfortunate circumstances or failures in life, stressing heredity, environment, or lack of opportunity. This attitude of mind sometimes acts as a temporary hypodermic to bolster lagging morale, but it does not get rid of the causes of suffering and affliction.

THE WORLD IS A MIRROR

Our world is a mirror reflecting our predominant mental attitude, and is constantly showing us ourselves. We do not always like what we see; neither do we regularly and systematically take the initiative and proceed to change the picture. If we indulge in negative tendencies, we soon come face to face with conditions of a similar vibration based on the fact that like attracts like. This is the perfect working of the law of cause and effect. We constantly deny that everything depends on cause, and with stupendous blindness we seek to change the effect.

A streak of jealousy aroused in us will indubitably attract situations involving other jealous people, either in the home, at business, or in our social world. Quite often we hear people say that the one thing they dislike most is jealousy in others. If we watch their reactions, we find the fault is in themselves. What we think or feel finds its affinity in our external world and finds its likeness.

LOOKING INSIDE OURSELVES

We must learn to take the beam out of our own eye by self-study, self-awareness, and self-examination. Eventually we shall not discern even the mote in our brother's eye. When we see faults in others, let us look inside ourselves, for there we shall find them, if we look with unbiased examination, hidden in the recesses of our own mind.

CHANGED ATTITUDES CHANGE EVERYTHING

If we constantly fail to achieve our goals in life and all our efforts meet a stone wall, we must look within and see why. To effect a change of circumstances and conditions in our lives, there must be a change of mental attitude, a mental acceptance dominated by the spirit of success along all lines. In order to succeed, we must realize that we are born to win and that the Infinite within us can't fail, knowing that we will generate the confidence of success, erasing from our mind every discordant thought. It is our mood, the intensity of sustained faith, which impresses itself on the subjective mind. The barrier to success is when we allow our personal ego to draw a boundary around our mentality.

SOME QUESTIONS

It is good to ask ourselves if we are simply seeking recognition and applause for ourselves, or if we are sincerely interested in serving humanity and making the world a better place in which to live. Do we want only to feather our own nest, or are we sincerely interested in what we are attempting to do for its own sake? Do we want to be an Emerson, a Lincoln, or an Edison who contribute to humanity in a wonderful way, or do we merely seek self-aggrandizement and personal glory?

If we have something to offer, it will be used unless we stand in its way. Vacillation, wavering, and so-called mercurial ups and downs result from a lack of an inner objective or ideal. Ofttimes a person says, "I am going around in circles." He hopes someone will come along eventually and show him how to extricate himself from the difficulty. Such a person lacks stability and does not know that there is an Infinite Intelligence within him Which, when called upon, would guide him and reveal to him the answer. *Speak, Lord; for thy servant heareth* (I Samuel 3:9).

6

The Meaning of Age-Old Truths

THIS WAS MY third visit to Bangkok, Thailand's fairytale city of temples and elaborate palaces, and I noticed a great number of changes, most of which were of a healthy nature. We went to the market by boat just as the Thais do. Gliding down the "klongs" (canals) to the floating market, we saw boats piled with vegetables and flowers.

It was also interesting to observe the saffron-robed monks out in the dawn collecting food in their begging bowls. It was fascinating to view the Temple of the Dawn as well as many other temples and palaces with their indescribable variety of Buddhas— gold ones, reclining ones, even an emerald one! The Temple of the Golden Buddha contains the largest, oldest Golden Buddha measuring ten feet in height and weighing five and one half tons. This represents a lot of gold!

The guide gave an interesting lecture on the topic of Buddhism and the many healings people receive when they pray and make their offerings at the shrine. A man in one group brought up the question of the Sphinx, asking what I thought about it from a religious standpoint. The idea came to me that it would be a good title for a section of this book.

THE SPHINX AND YOU

As for the likeness of their faces, they four had the face of a man, and the face of a lion, on the right side: and they four had the face of an ox on the left side; they four also had the face of an eagle (Ezekiel 1:10).

In the ancient Greek myth, the Sphinx propounded to all comers the riddle of man, and those who could not answer the riddle died. The riddle was: "What walks on four legs, on two legs, and on three legs?" The ancient answer was supposed to be man, because he crawls on hands and feet as a baby, then walks erect on two feet until such time as he uses a cane or crutch to help him when he gets very old and feeble.

This explanation, however, is not the correct one. The inner meaning is as follows: We must admit that most of the members of the human race are still walking on four legs, which means they are immersed in the mass mind and governed by the law of averages. The mass mind means the thoughts, feelings, beliefs, fears, superstitions, passions, prejudices, and false beliefs of four billion people.

There are, of course, a large number of people throughout the world who pray scientifically and who pour into the collective unconscious of the mass mind constructive, harmonious thoughts; but they are in the minority. Therefore, if we do not do our own thinking, each one of us must honestly ask himself: Is it the mass mind thinking in me or am I really doing my own thinking? To think is to compare. You choose thoughts based on eternal verities, truths which never change but are the same yesterday, today, and forever.

Think about whatever things are true, lovely, noble, and Godlike; then you are truly thinking. If there is any fear, worry, or anxiety in your thinking, it is the mass mind thinking in you. Millions of people have forgotten or are completely ignorant of the laws of mind and the way of the Spirit in man.

The four-footed animal is the five sense man who lives to eat and enjoy the pleasures of the flesh. The symbol of the four-footed animal also means the materialistic type of man who walks the earth believing only what he sees and who thinks that his security rests in the accumulation of riches and things of the world. He is the type of man who has forgotten to lay up treasures in heaven by the contemplation of the truths of God from the highest standpoint.

Symbolically speaking, not too many men and women are walking erect who have discarded animal propensities and tendencies; and of those who have spiritually matured, only a small minority walk the earth bearing all their weight on the crutch of intuition or inspiration from the Higher Self.

The symbolism of the Tarot Card "The Wheel of Fortune" is an adaptation of the vision in the first chapter of Ezekiel, which is considered one of the most occult chapters in the Bible—the four sacred animals and the wheels within wheels. . . . *And they four had one likeness: and their appearance and their work was as it were a wheel in the middle of a wheel* (Ezekiel 1:16).

The four wheels indicate the four planes, which are spiritual, mental, emotional, and physical; or the four stages of an idea, which are Consciousness, Awareness, the I AM within you, desire, feeling the reality of it, and the manifestation; or the four stages of the seed, which are the seed, the soil, the creative essence, and the plant.

Symbolically, the four mentioned in the Bible—the man, the lion, the ox, and the eagle—represent the four fixed signs of the Zodiac, which are Taurus, Leo, Scorpio, and Aquarius. The four mentioned also represent the four letters in the name Jehovah, I.H.V.H. The first letter, Yod, means God, I AM, or Unconditioned Consciousness, Spirit, the Source of all life. The second letter, HE, represents your desire, the thought-image in your mind, your clarified mental picture. The third letter, Vau, symbolizes feeling, love, emotion; i.e., you pour life into your idea, and in that manner you subjectify it and make it real. The fourth letter, HE, is the manifestation of what you imagined and felt to be subjectively true. This is the way all things come to pass in your world.

All these symbols refer to the fourfold constitution of man and are referred to as the four beasts of Revelation. Leo represents the lion, or Spiritual power. Taurus means the bull, the beast of burden, as we labor with our desire to till the soil of our mind and deposit our thought-image in our subconscious mind. Aquarius signifies the water bearer. Water means psychological truths, which means we meditate on the reality of our desire by pouring water, or feeling, on our ideal.

We imagine the happy ending, remaining loyal and devoted to our ideal. Scorpio (eagle) means the impregnation of our subconscious mind, or the finished state. These four fixed signs of the Zodiac can also be explained in this manner: consciousness or Spirit (I AM), desire, feeling the reality of it, and realization.

How to Test Your Desire

There is an urge towards growth and expansion in every human being. It is Life seeking expression through you. Your desire to give more of life, love, truth, and beauty is laudable and desirable. Your desire to be greater than you are is a normal and natural desire. If you are a musician, you desire to release more wonderful music which would stir the souls of men. Any desire that contributes to your health, happiness, peace, or welfare is good and very good. When your desires are lifeward, when they contribute to your spiritual and mental expansion, they are good and of God.

Your desire should never be to take advantage of others or interfere with the other's welfare or growth in any way whatsoever. Swedenborg said, "The essence of hell is the desire to rule over others." Desire to give out more life, love, and goodwill. The more you give, the more you will have. Desire to give more abundantly of the Life Force within you. Pour life and love into your ideals which are constructive.

Anything in the world that contributes to your welfare, success, and happiness must of necessity be a blessing to others because we are all one. The more goodwill, the more laughter, the more joy you give to others, the more you have. Your desire for wealth, promotion, and expansion in your field, whether professional or in business, is normal and natural. But be sure you look to God, not man, as the Source of all blessings.

Claim your good in Divine law and order. There are millions of channels, but only One Source. Always go to the Source, for everything you want. The innermost nature of being is the tendency of giving. Thus, if you have any doubt as to the nature of your own desires, test them for the quality of giving. Will the fulfillment of your desire contribute to your well-being? Will it enable you to express more of life, love, and energy?

The Divine Energy came to earth in order, the gospel story says, that we might have life and have it more abundantly. . . . *I am come that they might have life, and that they might have it more abundantly* (John 10:10). This desire to give of your talents, your abilities, your love, your geniality, your cordiality, and goodwill will never be disappointing. All this is backed on the age old truth: "The more you give, the more you have."

Your desire "to be"—the great healer, the great physician, the great teacher, the great singer, to express yourself at your highest level and to give light to all those around you—is God-like, good, and very good.

GETTING A NEW HALO

God indwells all men. Some men are expressing more of their Divinity than others, however. A man may fail and fall, but he cannot forfeit his Divinity. It is untouchable. The poorest slouch you see on the street is a manifestation or expression of God, and nothing can stop his eventual unfoldment.

Jesus saw this, regardless of the hash about an everlasting hell which His followers made out of His teaching. He castigated and criticized nobody but hypocrites. He did not in the least object to keeping what hypocrites called bad company. Neither did Buddha. They each recognized that in all people—be they scoundrels or saints—the Presence of God resides.

Exalt God in the midst of you. Do this many times a day. Also salute the Divinity in every person you meet. As you do this, the glory of God will shine more and more through you, for there is no end to the glory which is man.

WHEELS WITHIN WHEELS

Your concept or estimate of yourself determines the circle of friends you have, your social and professional status, your financial state and all phases of your life. You can constantly enlarge that circle by getting a greater concept of yourself and by extending your horizons. The diameter determines the circumference of a circle. Your diameter is your real estimate of yourself.

How much are you worth mentally, spiritually, and in your knowledge of the laws of mind? All of us are living in different worlds based on our early training, indoctrination, beliefs, opinions, theological conditioning, etc. All of us look out through the contents of our own mentality, and we each see a different world. The world we see is the world we are.

Each one of us has his own private world of thoughts, opinions, beliefs, and imagery. The radio engineer tells us that he can send program after program on one beam and they do not collide with each other because they are sent on different frequencies. It is my understanding that many transatlantic messages over the coaxial cables of the telephone company can be sent at the same time at different frequencies.

There may be five members of your family; yet each one is living in his or her own private world—a wheel within a wheel. One scientist said there were about an octillion number of electrons in our body (our body is composed of electrons, protons, atoms, molecules), but each atom or molecule is a world in itself.

The difference between one metal and another is based on the number and rate of motion of electrons revolving around a nucleus. Look at a bar of silver or gold. When examined under the eyes and ears of scientific instruments, they are not solid at all but are composed of billions of little worlds within the bar of silver, gold, or steel.

Physicians know that the cells composing your eyes are different than bone cells, and the cells of your heart are entirely different than the cells of your intestinal tract. Each cell functions according to its nature, however, and is a world within itself. For example, the cells in your bronchi cannot do the work of your liver, your heart, or your digestive system.

Your body is a complex compound of atoms and molecules.

Actually, and more basically, it is composed of waves of light. Furthermore, you have another body within the one you now have. It is called a subtle body, a fourth-dimensional body or astral body, which means that you can leave your present body and appear in any part of the world. You will have bodies to Infinity, and you will never be without a body, for a body is necessary for the expression of Spirit.

Each one of us is projecting outwardly on to other people, circumstances, and events the world of his beliefs, feelings, and emotional conditioning. Two women may look at a drunkard in the gutter. That does not mean that the women are drunkards; it means the way they feel inside colors what they see on the outside. One woman has compassion for him and realizes the Presence of God within him and calls It forth. The other woman says, "They should experiment with new drugs on him rather than on guinea pigs." She denounces him bitterly. Both see the same man, but they react differently. We likewise project onto others our emotions, temperament, and inner conditioning.

To Be and to Do

Suppose, for instance, that your main desire in life is to become a great singer who will bring joy to thousands or even millions through your singing. Sit quietly two or three times a day, shut out the evidence of senses, and imagine you are singing before a multitude. Claim that God is singing majestic cadences through you, which stir the hearts of people everywhere. Feel the naturalness of it. Hear a loved one congratulate you on your marvelous success.

As you meditate in this manner, you will discover that the time will come when this state of mind is fixed in your subconscious mind and that all the qualities and attributes necessary will be resurrected, as they were always within you in the first place. Remember, the Sphinx is within you. It is your Unconditioned Consciousness, the Unconditioned Awareness, the God within you.

This is the center, or Sphinx, around which all things revolve. It is the Unmoved Mover of all, while the world, galaxies of space and the wheel of personalities ceaselessly turn beneath the One Who Forever Is. You condition the unconditioned by claiming and feeling you now are what you long to be. As you remain faithful to that mental image, you will experience the joy of the answered prayer.

BANDS OF LOVE

. . . But they knew not that I healed them. I drew them with cords of a man, with bands of love . . . (Hosea 11:3-4). In order to form this perfect circle, you must think in harmony with the Infinite Presence and Power. This is sometimes called being "in tune with the Infinite." We are not compelled to love, but we have freedom to love.

Love is spontaneous and joyous, and we have the ability to give or to withhold it. There is no compulsion to love. For example, there would be no joy unless we could experience the opposite. How could you experience joy unless you had known sorrow? Love must be freely bestowed. Someone may feign love due to necessity or a sense of dependency, but this is not love. When our thoughts are in tune with the Infinite, they form a perfect circle or circuit and return to us, pressed down, shaken together, and running over.

When our thoughts are negative, as when, for example, we indulge in criticism, jealousy, or feeling sorry for ourselves or another, we are not in tune with God; consequently, there is no polarity. The circle of good is not formed.

The remedy for problems is to realize that the seat of Omnipotence is within us. By quietly stilling the mind, we realize gently that all power and energy necessary to overcome any situation, be it what it may, are ours now. A battery is formed by connecting opposite poles of zinc and copper, causing a circuit, which generates energy. This identical process is repeated when we meditate. Our thoughts must be charged with energy or emotionalized by love. In other words, we must become one with our ideal by feeling the reality of the state desired within ourselves. This is the polarization of thought, or the wheel within wheels.

YOU CAME FROM EDEN

THOU HAST BEEN in Eden the garden of God; every precious stone was thy covering . . . (Ezekiel 28:13). You were in Eden, or the paradisiacal state, the absolute state of all bliss, before you were born. In other words, you were Spirit. Your father and mother, during coition, struck a certain note and the Spirit, or the Absolute, became relative and was conditioned through your parents as you. We are wheels within the one wheel—the Motionless One—yet, all motion takes place within It.

What is a day? a month? a year? a lifetime? a thousand lifetimes? Time ceases for those who turn within to the Timeless One and tap the wisdom, the power, and the glory within. Deep within us is something that reminds us of our origin and urges us back to It. Our mission and purpose in this life is to cherish, enlarge, and glorify this memory, to follow sincerely that inner impulse until the spark grows by cultivation into a light which fills us, and we identify ourselves with It.

Eve, the subconscious of man, was taken from the rib while he slept. This is, of course, an allegory. The true meaning is as follows: It is during sleep that the subconscious emerges. She comes forth from the rib. The symbology of the ribs is protective, as the ribs protect the vital organs of the body. This merely portrays the protective nature of the subconscious.

During sleep Eve takes the office of instructor. The subconscious feeds the body and carries on the internal process of which the conscious mind is wholly unaware. It is said that Eve was made subject to man for good or evil. Our subconscious is subject to the conscious mind. We have defiled it, however. In the same way that we have degraded and abused it, though, we can purify it by our thoughts and moods.

Wives, submit yourselves unto your own husbands . . . (Ephesians 5:22). The wife in the Bible is your subconscious mind, and the husband is the conscious mind. Psychologically speaking, the subconscious (wife) is subject to the conscious mind (husband). This, of course, is not true in their personal relationship. All of us operate the male and female principle within us.*

In the ancient Tarot teaching, the Hebrew mystic said, "Subservient was she to be to her husband all the days of her life." At night the subconscious takes charge; and, according to your mood prior to falling asleep, you experience joy (if your thoughts are of the good and beautiful), or you have unpleasant experiences, particularly if you have gone to sleep in a turbulent mood. In this latter case Eve (your subconscious) is simply pointing out to you that you have mismanaged things. She also instructs and guides you and says what she pleases.

By filling your mind with the eternal verities and by busying your mind with the concepts of peace, harmony, right action, and goodwill to all, you will succeed in eradicating all the doubts, fears, and other negative states that may be lurking in your subconscious due to past errors and superstitions. Your subconscious may warn you in a dream. For example, if you are fearing a certain disease, your subconscious may dramatize your fear when asleep, showing you in the hospital, attended by doctors and nurses.

Now, there is no such thing as an inexorable fate. The dream mentioned can easily be explained. Your subconscious reasons deductively only and deduces a conclusion from the fear of disease entertained by you and magnifies this fear in a dream. You can change the dream and neutralize the fear by

---

* See the chapter on "The Bible and Woman's Bondage" in *Great Bible Truths for Human Problems* by Dr. Joseph Murphy, DeVorss and Company, Inc., Marina del Rey, California, 1976.

contemplating the wholeness, beauty, and perfection of God saturating your whole being and realizing that God in the midst of you is healing you now. Rejoice and give thanks for the Infinite Healing Presence operating in you now. Saturate your mind with these truths prior to sleep and your subconscious will respond accordingly.

7

Peace in This Changing World

WHEN WE ARRIVED at Singapore, referred to frequently as "the crossroads of the Orient," the guide conducted us through the famous waterfront, beautiful temples, Chinatown, Tiger Balm Gardens, and the House of Jade. It is most interesting to perceive and meditate on all the racial and cultural diversity of the unique city of Singapore.

Here you will see many picturesque Malay villages nestling in among coconut plantations operated by Malay, Chinese, and Indian workers. The House of Jade, which we visited, contains one of the world's finest jade collections.

Singapore River is an extraordinary sight packed with sampans, boats of all descriptions, and laborers on the docks bearing cargo on bare shoulders.

On a tour of the Singapore harbor, we enjoyed listening to the old man guiding the boat, and his grandson. They chanted prayers all the way back and forth. The prayers were from the

Koran. Both seemed ecstatic as they sang aloud the age-old sayings from their sacred Book.

We had a wonderful guide who was well acquainted with the laws of mind. He said that in the town of his birth in India there was much injustice, dishonesty, and corruption and that the people had put up with it for a long time. When a young girl was molested on her way to school, however, the people became incensed and threw the local politicians out of office.

His father was, as he said, the "first to stick his neck out" based on the old adage, "The turtle goes forward only when his neck is out." When these people became disturbed and agitated enough by the gross corruption and the prevalence of houses of ill fame in their neighborhood, they rose up in indignation and changed things.

You must realize that you, too, can become greater, grander, nobler, and more God-like than you are. This guide had been dissatisfied with the lack of opportunities of his birthplace. He was disturbed and he did something about it. He left the country, saying to himself, "I am going to travel, learn foreign languages, and get a college education." Having made up his mind and coming to a decision, his subconscious opened up the way, and he achieved the desire of his heart and found peace in this changing world.

DISSATISFACTION LEADS TO SATISFACTION

The author was also completely dissatisfied with the orthodox teaching he had received as a boy and later he revolted against it. He threw the entire teaching of early childhood overboard and found satisfaction in the laws of mind and the way of the Infinite Spirit. All Its ways are pleasantness and all Its paths are peace. He was disquieted and perturbed by false doctrines and illogical, unreasonable, and unscientific dogmas and false beliefs about God, life, and the universe.

He decided to write books clarifying life and its purpose. Today there are about thirty-two books which he has published, many of which have been translated into a number of foreign languages. It is good at times to be vexed, perplexed, annoyed, and disturbed, as it may cause you to do something constructive about it. Then you will find that inner peace and satisfaction.

WHY HE WROTE A BOOK

The late Dr. Harry Gaze, author of several books on the mind, told me that he was bothered and pestered in his lectures all over the world by people asking him about death, afterlife, and judgment. Being discommoded by all these questions, he wrote a book entitled *You Live Forever*, which became immensely popular. He said that he worked off all his tension in writing the book and consequently felt a great inner satisfaction. He got people to realize that there was no death—only life—and that God is life and God cannot die. His life is your life now.

YOU CAN FIND PEACE

In the Book of Matthew we read: *Think not that I am come to send peace on earth: I came not to send peace, but a sword. For I am come to set a man at variance against his father, and the daughter against her mother, and the daughter in law against her mother in law. And a man's foes shall be they of his own household* (Matthew 10:34–36).

Some time ago I gave a lecture in which I stated that the Virgin Mary meant the "I AM" within us capable of infinite conceptions of Itself—that it meant literally the pure sea. *Mare* means the sea; the word *Virgin* in the Bible means pure and undefiled—that it had the same meaning as Isis, the Goddess of 10,000 appellations; Maya, the mother of Buddha; Sophia of the Persians—and that the word antedated Christianity. This disturbed several in the audience. They were quite perturbed and agitated.

I explained to them that offtimes truth hurts because it shakes them up out of the doldrums of dead dogma and theological complexities. They began to do research work and discovered that all the characters of the Nativity are within every man. Furthermore, these young ladies got intensely interested in the science of the mind and have transformed their lives as a result. They said to me that they were glad I had stirred them up from their smugness, complacency, and lethargy.

A great number of people need to be disturbed and shaken up out of the mass propaganda, hypnotic suggestions, and false beliefs which are rampant in the field of religion. The above young women have discovered the Presence of God within themselves and have found peace in this changing world.

Tranquilizers Won't Give You Peace

A young actress phoned me terribly agitated and fear-stricken, stating that a palm reader had told her that someone had placed a curse upon her and that for $100 she could remove it. Having paid the fee, she seemed to get worse, however, and her physician prescribed a powerful tranquilizer. In her own words, she felt like a walking zombie.

I explained to her that she had to eradicate the cause. I pointed out to her that the imprecations of others had no power whatever to disturb her, that the suggestions and statements of others could not affect her—that the only power was the movement of her own thought. She had accepted the negative suggestion of the palm reader, and the whole reaction from which she was suffering was due to the movement of her own mind.

Under direction she began to recite slowly, quietly, and reverently the words of the 91st Psalm, the great protective Psalm of the Bible, which has saved people all over the world from shipwrecks, fires, incurable conditions, and hopeless situations.

She began to be aware of some simple truths. She knew that as she tuned in with the Infinite Presence and Power, Which is the only Power, It would move as harmony, peace, love, joy, beauty, and power through her. There is nothing to oppose this Presence, since It is Omnipotent. This realization gave her a sense of inner peace.

She blessed the palm reader and radiated love and goodwill to all, knowing that when she poured out love, goodwill, cordiality, and blessings to all, she would build up a wonderful immunity and become free. She found the peace that passeth understanding. She laughed at the negative suggestion of the palm reader, who had no more power than a pea shooter aimed at a British battle ship. She threw away the tranquilizers which she no longer needed. She did something about her suffering and pain and found peace within.

She Thought She Had to Put Up with It

A few months ago a woman came to see me. During the conference that ensued, she said that she had been told she had to suffer and put up with her arthritis as there was no cure. She was taking twelve to fourteen aspirin tablets a day, which had some unpleasant side effects in her case. She had then resorted to codeine tablets to alleviate the pain. Her relatives told her that it was the will of God and that she should bear the pain stoically. This, of course, is nothing but a diabolical perversion of the Truth, which states, *Come unto me, all ye that labour and are heavy laden, and I will give you rest* (Mathew 11:28). . . . *I am the Lord that health thee* (Exodus 15:26).

Pain is a blessing in disguise, because it calls to our attention the fact that we have misused our mind and should correct it at once. She was beginning to accept the lie and resign herself to her fate until the irritation of the pain became so excruciating that she decided to use and invoke Divine healing. Her frustration became so intense that she decided to reject the suggestions of others and do something about it.

In talking with her, I discovered that she was a seething

cauldron inside, harboring a deep-seated hatred and a festering resentment toward her ex-husband and mother-in-law. At my suggestion, she came to a definite decision and began to appraise herself as a spiritual being, a daughter of the Infinite, and a child of Eternity. Three times a day she sat down quietly for fifteen or twenty minutes and affirmed feelingly and knowingly: "God is Love, and God's love saturates my soul. I exalt God in the midst of me, and I give thanks for my miraculous healing now." When thoughts of hostility toward her ex-husband or mother-in-law came to her mind, she immediately affirmed, "God's love fills my soul," thereby neutralizing and chopping the head off every angry or hateful thought.

At the end of three months the suppleness and mobility of her joints returned and she walked without a cane. She is now free from all pain. She had tried previously to coerce her mind to love her ex-husband and mother-in-law and had got nowhere. But as she began to give her subconscious a Divine transfusion of love, peace, and harmony, the healing love of God dissolved all the calcareous deposits in her joints. Furthermore, as she began to appraise herself as a spiritual being and as she began to let in the sunshine of God's love, all hatred and hostility disappeared, being expunged from her deeper mind. She could, therefore, meet her former so-called enemies in her mind and no more sting was felt. She was at peace.

He Said, "Of Course I Am Tense"

While talking with a musician recently, he said, "I feel very tense before I play. If I am not full of tension before I play, I don't give an excellent performance." He said that in the beginning an associate of his told him to take a tranquilizer to relieve his nervous tension; but, after following the advice, his performance was very poor. He said he then realized, "It was tension that was necessary to make me excel in my music."

He said, "Now I get tense to a point similar to a wound-up watch. Then I tick off the excess energy and play. I am careful not to get over-tense and do not wind the watch to the point where I break the spring." This musician is wise. He likens his performance to the coiled spring of his Geneva watch, which releases the tension slowly causing the watch to operate. This stage musician realized that sedatives and tranquilizers were not the answers to his high tension. On the contrary, his high tension was simply an accumulation of Divine energy, enabling him to release the imprisoned splendor within him. This man had tension under his control and released it in Divine law and order. He thus found peace and serenity.

How He Released High Tension

A young medical student told me that he used to get so angry and upset with his relatives, with whom he was boarding while attending medical school, that he painted their faces on a punching bag in the college athletic quarters. He punched the pictures of each of them regularly every day for a half an hour, giving about five minutes to each.

He claimed that this released his pent-up emotions and prevented his exploding in a fit of rage in their presence. I explained to him that the more anger and hostility he hurled at them by punching the bag, the worse he would get. In other words, he would magnify the negative emotions within himself.

If it were true that all he had to do to get rid of the emotions of hostility and anger was to express them, then the reverse would also be true: the way to get rid of love, peace, cordiality, and goodwill would be to express them. On the contrary, however, as we do this we grow in love, peace, harmony, and goodwill. Actually, the more we express these qualities, the more Godlike and spiritual we become. The qualities are of God, and the more we give of these qualities, the more we possess. The more wisdom you impart to others, the more you have.

It is a diabolical perversion of truth to tell a person who is full of hostility that the way to get rid of it is to express it. Actually, he begins to murder love, peace, harmony, and discernment within him. If he keeps it up, these emotions reach a point of saturation which destroy him. Accordingly, this young intern began to surrender all his relatives to God and practiced religiously blessing each one by affirming whenever he thought of any one of them, "I exalt God in the midst of you." As he made a habit of this, he attained an inner peace and his relatives no longer troubled or irritated him. He realized that he was irritating himself.

LOOK AT THE TREE

You will notice how sturdy the tree is. It bends with the breeze and usually withstands the storm. It does not break easily. Likewise, all of us should bend and be flexible in meeting the vicissitudes of life. Learn to roll with the blows, knowing that everything passes away and you can meet the problem head on. Realize and know in your heart that through the Creative Intelligence within you, the problem can be solved.

. . . *Stand still, and see the salvation of the Lord . . .* (Exodus 14:13).

THE CAUSE OF THE REVOLUTION

An internationally-known correspondent the other evening brought out the fact as to why there was strife, bombing, and warfare in a certain country. He pointed out that it was due to money. Certain men at the top were corrupt, dishonesty was rampant, and the man at the top had all his relatives on the payroll and exacted a tax on everything brought into the country. The opposing political party wanted some of the graft and the power. When it was refused, they started a civil war.

Great waste, bribery, corruption, high taxes, and dishonesty perturb the minds of men and women everywhere. Finally, when it gets to the point of saturation in their minds, they explode.

One of the passengers on the trip asked me why it is that the wealthy people in a certain city in India ignored the frightful squalor, filth, disease, and poverty-stricken children, obviously half-starved. The answer is that they are inured to it. They attribute the deplorable condition of these children to karma, meaning they are suffering because of former sins in a former lifetime, which is a dastardly belief. It also gives them the excuse for doing nothing. External conditions do not disturb these people. Their false religious beliefs appease their conscience.

LOWLY LISTENING

Emerson said that by lowly listening we can hear the whisper of the gods, which means that there is an intuitive voice in all of us which prompts us to do the right thing. There is that within us that tells us to rise, transcend, and grow. It reveals to us that there is something grander, greater, and more wonderful waiting for all of us.

The inner voice reveals a contrast between our outside condition and our heart's desire; then it creates tension and makes us uneasy. We are living in an inner world and an outer world. A simple way to illustrate this duality of our nature is as follows: that which I AM and that which I long to be create a quarrel in my mind. In other words, you and your desire. Your desire for wealth, prosperity, success, and the good things of life may contrast vividly with your environment, home life, and financial status.

It is your desire for better things and a better life that sets up the drive within you to rise up and move forward in life. You are here to grow, expand, and rise higher in all phases of your life. When you cease to dream, to aspire, to grow, and to give more of your talents and abilities to the world, you stagnate and die spiritually.

The Sword

When the Bible says, *I come as a sword*, it simply means that the sword severs. Symbolically, it separates the false from the real, the truth from the lie and the false, erroneous beliefs of the world. With the sword of truth, you detach yourself; you cut yourself off from the adhesions or erroneous concepts of God, and enable yourself to enthrone in your mind a God of love.

Truth creates a quarrel in your mind because it creates a conflict between what you have been taught and the actual truth of Being. However, the sword of truth resolves the quarrel as you accept the I AM—the Presence of God within you—as the only Presence, Power, Cause, and Substance. As you give all your allegiance, loyalty, and devotion to the Living Spirit Almighty within you, all the false gods fall away and peace enters your mind and heart.

A man may be at variance with his father in the sense that he no longer subscribes to his father's antiquated, perhaps grotesque and monstrously absurd religious beliefs about a God of wrath, hell's fire, and brimstone, sinners in the hands of an angry God, salvation, original sin, savior, lake of fire, and a host of other shibboleths too absurd for words.

The same would apply to daughters who hear the Truth, which sets them free from all fear. Any religion which instills fear into the mind must be false. . . . *I will fear no evil: for thou art with me* . . . (Psalm 23:4). *Fear not, little flock; for it is your Father's good pleasure to give you the kingdom* (Luke 12:32).

Your religion should give you joy, happiness, peace, and security. . . . *I am come that they might have life, and that they might have it more abundantly* (John 10:10).

Many people are lazy, indolent, smug, lethargic, and exist in a pseudo-peace. They need the sword of Truth to stir them out of their lethargic state.

I come not to bring peace but a sword is a profound Truth. The awareness of the Presence of God in you is that which comes into your mentality for the purpose of transforming your whole life. The inner voice says to you: "Come on up higher. I have need of you." It wakes you up.

The sword of Truth is Divine reasoning whereby you reject everything in your mind that does not conform to the eternal verities and principles of life. You reason from the standpoint of the principles of harmony, love, peace, right action, and truths which never change. You reject all error as being unfit for the house of God. In other words, you follow the biblical injunction: *Judge not according to the appearance, but judge righteous judgment* (John 7:24).

HE DISCARDED THE TRUTH

An irate woman phoned me saying that one of her relatives was contesting the will of her late husband. Her sister had made false allegations. She added that the attorney knew her sister was lying and was throwing the truth away. She said that he was building a case upon a tissue of lies and false allegations.

I suggested that she remain calm, cool, and collected, however, and let the God-Self within her win the decision for her. She was to reject completely the idea of her sister having any power or her attorney having any power; her uplifted vision would prevail.

Accordingly, she prayed as follows: "The Truth of God prevails. Divine justice reigns supreme in the minds and hearts of all. It is God in action." She adhered to this uplifted state of consciousness. When fear came to her mind or false oaths were given by her sister, she would silently affirm, "It is God in action." The case was dismissed and her husband's will was carried out as specified.

The God-Presence in all of us comes bearing a sword urging us forward, onward, and upward. The Spirit (God) in you is always prodding you to go forward bearing the lamp of Truth and the balm of peace.

WEARING THE RIGHT SPIRITUAL GARMENTS

Enter into his gates with thanksgiving, and into his courts with praise . . . (Psalm 100:4). You should wear the proper mental garments of faith, confidence, goodwill, and the spirit of forgiveness and live in the joyous expectancy of the best. As you do, invariably, the best will come to you.

On visiting a psychiatric institution some months ago, a young intern pointed out some men who were always tearing off their clothes and insisting on walking around naked. The reason for this tendency is that they are mentally and spiritually naked. They have no covering for their minds, such as love, peace, harmony, and wisdom. As the young doctor pointed out, they are no longer using their intellect or the faculties of discernment and reason; consequently, their brains and other organs are rapidly disintegrating.

One insisted he was Caesar, another Lincoln, and another Washington. The gangsters of hate, jealousy, envy, and vengeance enthroned in their minds were the devils which caused them to lose the government of their minds, robbing them of peace, harmony, and health. This young physician said their irrational emotions were the cause of their insanity.

He brought out an interesting point when he informed me that a sister of one of these so-called lunatics visited every day. She kept telling him that the Light of God would dispel the darkness of his mind. Most of the time he didn't recognize her and paid little attention to her. She told the doctor she was practicing absent treatment for him by constantly realizing, "The Light of God shines in my brother's mind making him whole."

Three months went by; then one morning as she visited him, he spoke calmly to her and said the Light had come into his mind—a bright light—and that he was healed. Psychiatrists checked him and he was released. He has found peace within this changing world. His sister's conviction of the healing power of God was communicated to him subconsciously and he was made whole.

"More things are wrought by prayer than this world dreams of."

8

The Real Meaning of "You Are What You Eat"

A VISIT TO Hong Kong is something to remember. This was my fourth visit to this picturesque British Crown Colony perched on the edge of the Chinese mainland. As the plane prepares to land, one looks down on one of the most beautiful harbors of the world.

Hong Kong is fascinating and colorful, teeming with people, crammed with all kinds of bargains, clinging to its rock at the edge of the sea. The refugee problem is controlled much better now than it was during my visit some years previously. Government houses have been built for the unfortunate people and facilities for education have been provided.

We were also taken on a tour of Kowloon and the new territories. We drove past ancient walled villages and right up to the Bamboo Curtain. Cruising in the harbor on a Chinese junk is a unique experience. The fishing village of Sherdein, formerly a pirates' haunt, is most interesting. Dinner was served there on a floating restaurant.

Ye are the children of the Lord your God: ye shall not cut yourselves, nor make any baldness between your eyes for the dead.

For thou art an holy people unto the Lord thy God, and the Lord hath chosen thee to be a peculiar people unto himself, above all the nations that are upon the earth.

Thou shalt not eat any abominable thing.

These are the beasts which ye shall eat: the ox, the sheep, and the goat,

The hart, and the roebuck, and the fallow deer, and the wild goat, and the pygarg, and the wild ox, and the chamois.

And every beast that parteth the hoof, and cleaveth the cleft into two claws, and cheweth the cud among the beasts, that ye shall eat.

Nevertheless these ye shall not eat of them that chew the cud, or of them that divide the cloven hoof; as the camel, and the hare, and the coney: for they chew the cud, but divide not the hoof; therefore they are unclean unto you.

And the swine, because it divideth the hoof, yet cheweth not the cud, it is unclean unto you: ye shall not eat of their flesh, nor touch their dead carcase.

These ye shall eat of all that are in the waters: all that have fins and scales shall ye eat:

And whatsoever hath not fins and scales ye may not eat; it is unclean unto you.

Of all clean birds ye shall eat.

But these are they of which ye shall not eat: the eagle, and the ossifrage, and the osprey.

And the glede, and the kite, and the vulture after his kind,

And every raven after his kind,

And the owl, and the night hawk, and the cuckow, and the hawk after his kind,

The little owl, and the great owl, and the swan,

And the pelican, and the gier eagle, and the cormorant,

And the stork, and the heron after her kind, and the lapwing, and the bat.

And every creeping thing that flieth is unclean unto you: they shall not be eaten.

But of all clean fowls ye may eat.

Ye shall not eat of any thing that dieth of itself: thou shalt give it unto the stranger that is in thy gates, that he may eat it; or thou mayest sell it unto an alien: for thou art an holy people unto the Lord thy God. Thou shalt not seethe a kid in his mother's milk (Deuteronomy 14:1–21).

The idea for this chapter came to me while we were eating different kinds of fish in the floating restaurant. A nurse at the table said, "We are what we eat." If a thing is true, there is a way in which it is true. When in the Bible the Lord's Prayer says, *Give us day by day our daily bread* (Luke 11:3), it is not talking about bread on the table. It is the bread of Heaven, which means to eat mentally of confidence, faith, goodwill, and laughter.

Man should feed on moods and emotions which animate, strengthen, and sustain him. It is true that we need food for the body, such as protein, vegetables, and all the minerals necessary to sustain life, which come from the soil. . . . *Man shall not live by bread alone . . .* (Luke 4:4). He must have ideas which heal, bless, inspire, elevate, and dignify his soul. How can a man live without a modicum of peace, harmony, love, faith in God and all things good?

Our mind must be nourished. When the mind becomes charged with fear, anxiety, worry, and foreboding, these emotions bring on all kinds of misery and suffering. Man needs to live in the joyous expectancy of the best. Then he will discover that invariably and ineluctably the best will come to him. We get what we expect in life. Expect the highest and the best. Never settle for the second best.

How often have you risen from the banquet table, which was full of delicious food, yet remained hungry for love, peace, inner joy or longed for some kind of indescribable satisfaction which the food on the table did not or could not provide? *Blessed are they which do hunger and thirst after righteousness: for they shall be filled* (Matthew 5:6). Realize that your spiritual heritage has equipped you with all the powers and capacities needed to win and lead a triumphant life.

Better is a dinner of herbs where love is, than a stalled ox and hatred therewith (Proverbs 15:17). You can eat the choicest of food; and if you are angry, resentful, or hateful, the food will be transmuted into poison. There is nothing good or bad, but thinking makes it so.

A Japanese doctor present at our table in one of the hotels in Hong Kong said that since World War II the Japanese have been eating a lot of wheat, and that due to the vitamins in the wheat, the Japanese people are growing taller. The contents of our bodies consist of not only seventy-five to eighty percent water, but also a vast number of chemicals derived from the soil and protein from the meat. The soldier on a long march on a hot day knows the importance of sodium chloride, or salt. Potassium, iodine, and other chemicals are also essential for our welfare and health.

Food, of course, is important, but not preeminently so. We must not forget the Source of all food—the Life Principle within, which creates all things. Look to the Creator; not to the created thing. In other words, we must not look just to food for our health. We must realize: . . . *I am the Lord that healeth thee* (Exodus 15:26). The Bible says: . . . *According to your faith be it unto you* (Matthew 9:29).

Recently I talked with a woman who specialized in diet for a major hospital. She was a dietician and had college degrees in that specialty; yet she suffered from chronic arthritis as well as cancer of the womb. She freely admitted that her mental food had been resentment, hostility, and suppressed rage toward her ex-husband. As she began to appraise herself from a spiritual standpoint, however, recognizing her Divine heritage, the suppleness and mobility of her joints returned and the malignant tumor dissolved completely. She prayed for her doctor, and he reversed his method of treatment, which also helped her considerably.

Her main prayer was: "God in the midst of me is healing me now. His love fills every atom of my being." She affirmed this simple truth many times a day. When resentment or anger came to her mind, she would say to herself, "God's love fills my soul and He maketh me perfect now." She did not try to coerce herself to love her ex-husband, but she knew that as she filled her subconscious with God's love, all resentment, hostility, and hatred would be dissolved (and, of course, it was). Love casts out everything unlike itself. After a few weeks of this spiritual therapy, she could think of him and there was no longer any sting felt. She was at peace and is now free from cancer and arthritis.

The body moves as it is moved upon. The body acts as it is acted upon. She played a melody of love on her body instead of a hymn of hate, and the body responded. Spirit and matter are one. Your body is the manifestation of Spirit, or God. Your thought patterns represent the mediator between the Invisible Spirit and the manifested state.

The Book of Deuteronomy, Chapter 14, which we are writing about here, is one of the most important in the Bible. It tells you in the first verse that you are a child of the Infinite and that you shall not cut yourself. This means you should not inflict mental traumas on yourself, such as self-condemnation, hate, fear, resentment, etc., as all these are wounds to your soul, or subjective mind, and may become festering poison pockets in the recesses of your deeper mind, sending psychic pus all over your system.

For thou art an holy people unto the Lord thy God. . . (Deuteronomy 14:2). The Holy One is within you. Because It is perfect, whole, all harmony, perfect peace, boundless love, and infinite intelligence, all Its purposes are synchronized and functioning perfectly in your body. God indwells you and is the Life Principle in you. It is whole, complete, and perfect in Itself. Holy means to make whole, i.e., we should function harmoniously and peacefully in all phases of our lives. The

Life Principle functions perfectly through us unless we interfere and intrude with or misuse the law.

Moses in the Bible represents the law of mind, which is: . . . *As he thinketh in his heart, so is he* . . . (Proverbs 23:7). In simple language this means that whatever a man impresses on his subconscious mind is expressed on the screen of space.

Thou shalt not eat any abominable thing (Deuteronomy 14:3). In other words, you must not mentally digest, absorb, or appropriate ideas and opinions which are negative and destructive. This is what is called "eating" in a biblical or mental or spiritual way. All of us are fed through the five senses morning, noon, and night. We hear, see, feel, taste, and touch all day long. We are impressed daily with an avalanche of sights and sounds, many of which are destructive and highly negative. Our real mental food or diet should be the eternal verities, or truths of God, which heal, bless, and inspire us. We are what we eat (think) all day long.

In a single day, our mind is receiving countless ideas, opinions, beliefs, and some truths, all of which impregnate our subconscious mind. These impressions and beliefs come forth as experiences and events in our lives. Our state of consciousness is the way we think, feel, believe, and whatever we give mental consent to. Our state of consciousness is our lord and master. Our ideal food should be to contemplate on all the qualities, attributes, and potencies of God, knowing that we become what we contemplate. Our mental state, which is our conditioned consciousness, may be mean, nasty, depressing, and spiteful, depending on the mental food appropriated by us.

When the Bible says *These are the beasts which ye shall eat* . . . (Deuteronomy 14:4), this is symbolic language. The word *beast* means emotion, animated states of mind. An animal does not reason critically like man. That is to say, an animal does not analyze, weigh, dissect, scrutinize, or investigate the pros and cons as a human being does. When we see a dog rescuing a drowning child or scraping away the snow where a man is buried alive in an avalanche, this indicates a degree of subjective reasoning. This sort of subjective or instinctive reasoning is observable also in many other animals. No animal can write the Sermon on the Mount or the Sermon at Benares, or write a Beethoven Sonata, or build a Gothic cathedral. Animals are governed by a subjective instinct and do not have the capacity to judge spiritually or practice Divine reasoning. They cannot grow spiritually and, therefore, cannot change their nature.

A drunkard, a dope fiend, or a murderer has the capacity to choose and come to a decision. Through the power of God he can lead a new life and move onward and upward. Man can redirect his emotional life. If he so desires, he can become a God-like man and experience what is called a spiritual rebirth. He is referred to as the renascent man. The abnormal or irrational emotions of anger, fear, hate, jealousy, hostility, etc., are called irrational emotions, as they are not based on Divine reasoning. . . . *Choose you this day whom ye will serve* . . . (Joshua 24:15).

We are here to choose; i.e., accept the good and reject the negatives of life. When we give power to externals and think that externals are causative, this attitude engenders anger and discordant emotions within, which play havoc with our lives. We are here to learn that externals are an effect—not causative— and that other people, conditions, and circumstances which suggest opposition have no power to hinder or thwart us in our ongoing.

The truth is: Omnipotence is within us, and as we join up with the Father within, realizing the God power is flowing on our behalf, we will keep our emotional life in harmony and peace. The mass mind moves in on all of us. That is why we must be constantly "prayed up." Stop and think of the false beliefs, false dogmas, and irrational and stupid concepts of God and the afterlife which were fed us when we were young. These impressions and fears are still lurking in the recesses of our subconscious mind. Biblically speaking, they are called unclean animals.

We can change our subconscious this moment by filling our minds with the truths of God, which crowd out of our mind everything unlike God. You are told in this biblical chapter that you can eat the ox, the sheep, the goat, and *every beast that parteth the hoof and cleaveth the cleft into two claws, and cheweth the cud among the beasts. That ye shall eat.*

It is necessary to understand the symbolical significance of these words. The greatest and foremost wisdom of the Bible can be understood only by the correct interpretation of the symbols incorporated throughout the Bible.

The cow and the sheep divide the hoof, which means that you are supposed to reason things out, separate the chaff from the wheat, the false from the real. In other words, you are to judge according to spiritual standards and principles of life and reject everything that is false and untrue. You must come to a decision on principles of life and choose the Truth, which never changes. You must no longer judge according to appearances. On the contrary, you judge according to eternal verities in the same manner as a mathematician comes to a conclusion regarding the principles of mathematics.

Having arrived at the truth, you must then chew the cud, which means that you meditate, think upon, assimilate, and appropriate that truth by digesting and absorbing it mentally so that it is incorporated into your subconscious mind and becomes a part of you in the same manner as an apple, when digested, becomes a part of your blood stream.

Reflect on the great truths of life. As you nourish and sustain them, you will become what you contemplate. This is the meaning of chewing the cud. Cows graze in the field and, when full, they lie down to ruminate. The grass which the cow has eaten goes from one stomach to the other. In the process of rumination, there is a casting up of incompletely digested food until it becomes a soft mass of chewed food called a bolus ready to be swallowed.

This is what you do when you really meditate. You mentally eat of the ideas you are contemplating. Then you are compelled to express what is incorporated into your subconscious mind. For example, you might get one hundred percent on an examination on metaphysics or philosophy by means of an intellectual dissertation on the subject; yet, you may not have absorbed it and integrated the truth into your heart. You failed to meditate on it, which means you didn't give the truth sufficient attention and devotion. You did not reflect long enough on the truth so that it was clear-cut in your understanding and thus became a living part of you.

The lips and the heart must agree. The brain and the heart must unite. Your conscious and subconscious must synchronize and agree. Then you have divided the hoof and you have chewed the cud, figuratively speaking. Then wonders happen in your life.

In verse 7 of the chapter we are discussing, it says you may not eat of the camel, the hare, and the coney, for they chew the cud but divide not the hoof. This is simple to understand: There are millions of people throughout the world who chew on all kinds of philosophies, teachings, and various religious cults but have never divided the hoof, i.e., they have never quietly reasoned things out and separated the mass mind's beliefs, dogmas, theories, and speculations from the Truth, which is always the same yesterday, today, and forever.

There is only One Truth, One Law, One Life, One God, the Father of all; and the basis of all religious beliefs, be they what they may, is this: *For as he thinketh in his heart, so is he* . . . (Proverbs 23:7). In other words, thoughts, ideas, and beliefs felt as true are deposited in the subconscious mind, and they come forth as experience, conditions, and events.

This law applies to all people throughout the world. It is not the thing believed in that matters; it is belief itself. Therefore, whether the object of your faith is true or false, you will get results. If you believe the bones of saints or the relics of a holy man will heal you, your subconscious belief will get results. It is not the bones or the relics. For example, if you substituted the bones of a so-called saint with the bones of a dog and the person touching them believed them to be the bones of a saint, he would get results due to his blind belief.

There are many people who chew the cud in another way. They say they are studying the science of the mind or the inner meaning of the Bible, and you find them delving into Ouija Boards for answers, studying numbers, the influence of the stars on their lives, seeking answers from departed spirits, etc. They are all muddled and confused for the simple reason that they have never really divided the hoof and come to a clear-cut decision that Truth is One and Indivisible.

The truth is: Your thought and feeling control your destiny. Your future is your present habitual thinking and imagery made manifest. The law of Life is the law of belief. Believe in the guidance of God, the goodness of God, the abundance of God and the love of God. Believe in Divine right action and Divine law and order. Believe in the principles of life and the response of Infinite Intelligence.

If you seek wisdom and solutions to your problems, go to God; don't seek answers from numbers, Ouija Boards, entities, cards, or departed spirits. *If any of you lack wisdom, let him ask of God, that giveth to all men liberally, and upbraideth not* . . . (James 1:5).

The unclean animals in the Bible represent false religious beliefs, which inhibit your growth and hold you in bondage and thralldom. False impressions control the minds of many people, and they are consequently leading very negative emotional lives. Reject all the false propaganda of the world; refuse to accept mentally anything unfit for the house of God, which you are. Reject unsavory food, such as negative suggestions of all kinds. The suggestions of others have no power to create. The creative power is in you—your own thoughts.

Cremate all negative thoughts with the fire of Divine love. Then you are dividing the hoof and chewing the cud. You are then a true meditator and dispenser of good. We are chewing the cud when we take the great truths of life, reflect on them, get absorbed and intensely interested to the point that they become integrated with our mentality and become a part of us. This is why Moses says you can eat the cow because she does both and is, therefore, clean.

The swine divides the hoof and chews not the cud; therefore, it is considered unclean. There are many people who know the truth; they take lessons in Unity, Science of Mind, and Divine Science and study psychology; yet they do not digest it or absorb it into their mentality. In other words, it is of the lips and they do not put it into practice. They merely talk about it and do not apply it in their daily lives. The truths of God must be incorporated into the subconscious mind; then we are compelled to express them. The law of the subconscious is compulsive.

The camel and the hare are unclean because these animals chew the cud and do not divide the hoof. All this means that people listen to all sorts of propaganda, try out all different religions, and study philosophies. They mix the good with the bad, and are constantly perplexed, confused, neurotic, and bottled up, so that fear is mixed with faith and goodwill with ill will; likewise, peace is mixed with pain.

You are told you can eat fish with fins and scales. Symbolically, this is a profound truth—one of the great allegories of the Bible. The scales represent protection; therefore, as you go through life, realize that you are watched over by the Overshadowing Presence of God and the whole armor of God surrounds you at all times. You will then lead a charmed life.

A fin is a membranous, winglike, or paddlelike appendage of an aquatic animal used in propelling the body. These types of fish steer themselves and are not subject to the tides and waves of the ocean like the helpless fish without these attachments. Oftentimes you see fish without fins and scales cast onto the beach, where they die.

When you have God as your guide and counsellor in life, you cease to drift because your master thought of God's guidance is in control, and you are led to ways of pleasantness and to paths of peace. It is well known that the salmon returns against all odds and the swiftest tides to the place of its birth. It has fins and scales.

When the suggestion of defeat, failure, and discouragement comes to the mind of a man who is full of confidence and faith, he grapples with the problem courageously and goes against the tide of depression and defeatism. He directs his mind toward the goal and desire of his heart, so he reaches the shore safely. He wins because the Infinite within him cannot fail.

Of all clean birds ye shall eat symbolically means we are like birds with two wings—the wings of thought and imagination. We can soar aloft above the storms, strife, and contentions of the world and rest in the Secret Place where all is bliss, harmony, and peace. Here we can abide beyond time and space, away from the opinions and verdicts of the world, and claim our good. The Spirit will honor and validate whatever image we claim and feel to be true.

We are told we shall not eat of the eagle, the ossifrage, the raven, the owl, and the hawk. These are birds of prey. Man must not prey on his fellow man. He must not rob, steal, cheat, or defraud others, for to steal from another is to steal from himself and attract loss and limitation. Actually, he impoverishes himself along all lines. The loss may come in many ways, such as loss of health, prestige, promotion, love, friends, etc.

Birds that feed on dead flesh are proscribed by Moses. Don't touch the dead past. The past is dead. Many people dwell mentally on old peeves, grudges, failures, losses, lawsuits, etc., and they reinfect themselves all over again. To indulge in jealousy, hatred or to desire to get even is decaying food, which robs you of health, vitality, and enthusiasm, and leaves you a physical wreck. This kind of mental food is poisonous. This is the reason Moses says, *You must not eat of the vulture, the hawk, . . .*

And every creeping thing that flieth is unclean . . . Many people crawl through life mentally eating of worldly beliefs, and fail to rise, transcend, and grow. We must leave the muddy and dusty thoughts of the world and ascend spiritually by recognizing that we are children of God and heir to all of God's riches. It is no use to fly with mud on our wings. We must be lifted up spiritually by the contemplation of the Presence of God.

Thou shalt not seethe a kid in its mother's milk is a Biblical statement of profound significance. A kid is a symbol of sacrifice, and milk is a symbol of nourishment and a universal food. The kid, when fed, grows up to be a goat and nobody wants to ride the goat. If, for example, you indulge in a deep-seated grudge or resentment, you are nourishing a mental poison that will grow up and expand into a growth or a tumor. You can't afford to seethe in anger or get all burned up, because you will become the goat and experience the result of your mental food. Feed on whatsoever things are lovely and of good report, and wonders will happen in your life.

9

The Biblical Meaning of The Strange Woman

THIS IS MY third visit to Japan, the home of the Seicho-No-Ie Movement, which means Infinite Life. It is headed by Dr. Masaharu Taniguchi, sometimes referred to as the Gandhi of Japan. The basic teaching is the same as that of the Laws of Mind, or Divine Science Movement in the United States. It could be called the New Thought Movement of Japan. New Thought in the United States is composed of Unity, Religious Science, Science of Mind, Divine Science, and Churches of Truth.

We went by jet to Osaka and then to Kyoto, which is one of the capitals of Ancient Japan. There we spent a thrilling time visiting the famous shrines, gardens, and palaces of graceful Kyoto. From Kyoto we drove to Nara, most ancient capital in Japan. We visited Totaji Temple with the tallest Buddha in the world, as well as the Kasuja Shrine. We had a "Bullet Train" ride from there through the picturesque Japanese countryside to the resort Stami and had the opportunity to see the awesome Buddha at Kamakura cast in 1252.

Tokyo is filled with exciting pleasures, including the Imperial Palace Plaza, National Diet Building, and Meiji Shrine. All of us enjoyed the tea ceremony and flower arranging at the famous Tea House.

It was in Tokyo that I got the idea for this chapter based on a question asked me by a student of Dr. Taniguchi. He was studying the esoteric meaning of the Old and New Testaments, and he asked me two questions: Why does the Bible talk about the strange woman, harlots, and prostitutes in the 7th Chapter of Proverbs? Why does the Book of Deuteronomy 23:2 say "A bastard shall not enter into the congregation of the Lord . . . "?

I think you will find that the explanations given in this chapter make sense. Essentially, these were the answers I gave to this young seminary student, who will be eventually a minister in Tokyo: Wedlock in the Bible means a mental and emotional union with the eternal verities—that which is lovely and of good report. A false belief born out of real wedlock is but a son of a harlot, which means undisciplined or negative emotions. A bastard idea is a false belief or the acceptance in your mind of untruths about God.

When you pray, you must know your Father and Mother God; or, in psychological language, you must know the interaction of your conscious mind (father) and subconscious mind (mother). When these two unite in harmony and peace, based on the truths of God, the children of that union are health, happiness, prosperity, wisdom, and understanding. The formula always is thought and emotion; the result is either good or bad, depending upon the nature of your thought.

For thou hast had five husbands . . . (John 4:18). In Isaiah 54:5, you are told: *Thy Maker is thine husband* . . . The five husbands are your five senses. It is very foolish to allow yourself to be impregnated with all the erroneous ideas, false propaganda, and fears generated by the masses. The offspring of the avalanche of sights and sounds and sundry propaganda of the media and the mass mind is not wholesome and is certainly unfit for the house of God (your mind).

Thy Maker means God, which means you should impregnate your conscious and subconscious with God-like thoughts and ideas which are noble, uplifting and God-like. In other words, you should think, speak, and act from the standpoint of eternal principles—the same way as a chemist thinks from the standpoint of the principles of chemistry. Then you have God for your husband in the sense that you think from the standpoint of Truth.

When you reach the stage where you sing the song of the jubilant soul, and when you constantly exalt the God Presence within, you have no further occasion to give birth to false ideas born of five-sense knowledge. You have arrived at the point where you contemplate the truths of God from the highest standpoint.

Say unto wisdom, Thou art my sister; and call understanding thy kinswoman:

That they may keep thee from the strange woman, from the stranger which flattereth with her words.

And beheld among the simple ones, I discerned among the youths, a young man void of understanding,

Passing through the street near her corner; and he went the way to her house,

In the twilight, in the evening, in the black and dark night:

And, behold, there met him a woman with the attire of an harlot, and subtil of heart.

(She is loud and stubborn; her feet abide not in her house:

Now is she without, now in the streets, and lieth in wait at every corner.)

So she caught him, and kissed him, and with an impudent face said unto him,

I have decked my bed with coverings of tapestry, with carved works, with fine linen of Egypt.

I have perfumed my bed with myrrh, aloes, and cinnamon.

Come, let us take our fill of love until the morning: let us solace ourselves with loves.

For she hath cast down many wounded: yea, many strong men have been slain by her.

Her house is the way to hell, going down to the chambers of death (Proverbs 7:4–5, 7–13, 16–18, 26–27).

Without allegory, you cannot understand life. *Without a parable spake he not unto them* (Matthew 13:34). We must see the inner meaning of these verses, which are of profound significance, teaching us how to use the laws of life. We must also understand symbols, as the greatest study of Truth is the study of symbols.

In essence, these verses from Proverbs tell you about a young man who was seduced by one of the ladies of the evening, which is nothing new, since it occurs all over the world every day. We must thoughtfully examine the Bible to perceive the wisdom the writer of Proverbs wishes to impart. Adultery is idolatry, the worship of false gods. When your mind cohabits with evil of any kind, you are committing adultery by introducing poisonous thoughts and false ideas into the sanctuary of God within you.

Committing Adultery

If you worship the stars and give power to them, you are saying that stars have power over you and are the cause of your misfortune. You are then committing adultery because you are making the created thing greater than the Creator. You are adulterating your mind by introducing opposition to the Infinite, Which is Omnipotent.

To resent, hate, to be jealous or envious is also to cohabit with evil. There is a waywardness of the mind as well as of the body. Actually, we are committing mental adultery when we unite with false beliefs of any kind.

Mental Marriages

All of us are performing mental marriages when we unite mentally and emotionally with any idea—good or bad—and, naturally, this union brings about corresponding offspring such as health or sickness, prosperity or poverty, joy or sadness. All this happens through the law of correspondence, which means that the mental equivalent is in our subconscious mind for everything that happens to us.

DANGER OF PROPAGANDA

You must discipline yourself to reject the suggestions and high-pressured propaganda drives regarding cancer, heart disease, etc. which appear on TV screens so frequently. Many people who do not discipline their minds create the very evil they fear. This is the result of an unholy marriage. Your thought and emotion bring forth a result, called the son or manifestation of the union.

We must be careful not to cohabit with the strange woman, such as fear, hate, jealousy, envy, or resentment, which results in all manner of sickness, lack, and limitation.

ARE YOU A VICTIM OF SUGGESTION?

This recent nation-wide scare of swine flu is another strange woman which has lured and seduced many people. According to the press, great numbers have suffered from paralysis and other serious side effects from the vaccine. The fear suggestions and propaganda regarding the swine flu had no power to affect you, however, except through your own thought. You could reject it completely and affirm an age-old truth: "I AM all health. God is my health."

Accept the truth of this statement and you render yourself immune to all this scare propaganda. A great number of outstanding medical men high in their professions have openly criticized the entire project.

YOUR TRUE WIFE

Your concept, estimate, and blueprint of yourself is what you are married to. Affirm the highest and the best and acknowledge that you are one with God, that God is your Father and your Mother, and that God loves you and cares for you. If you are a man, affirm boldly: "I AM a son of the Living God and I AM heir to all of God's riches." If a woman, affirm boldly: "I AM a daughter of the Living God and I AM heiress to all of God's riches." Wonders will happen in your life.

Whether a man or a woman, you are always marrying (accepting) some idea. The result of that mental and emotional union will come forth as form, experience, conditions, and events.

FALLING IN LOVE

Fall in love with (i.e., get married to) ideas which heal, bless, prosper, guide, inspire, strengthen, and lift you up. Busy your mind with these concepts, and you will leave no vacancy there for the false propaganda of the world. Marry Truth, which never changes, and health, prosperity, vitality, wisdom, and understanding will be your offspring.

Say unto wisdom, Thou art my sister; and call understanding thy kinswoman (Proverbs 7:4). Your sister is wisdom, which is an awareness of the Presence and Power of God in you. Understanding is to stand firmly on the Truth, knowing that whatever you claim and feel to be true, your subconscious will respond accordingly. Then you have found your true wife.

FAST AND PRAY

Is not this the fast that I have chosen? to loose the bands of wickedness, to undo the heavy burdens, and to let the oppressed go free, and that ye break every yoke? (Isaiah 58:6).

The oppressed are your unfulfilled desires and unattained ideals in life. We let them go free by realizing that God flows through us, filling up all the empty vessels in our lives. It is as easy for God to do this as it is to make a blade of grass.

The yoke that we break refers to the fears and limitations held in our subconscious mind. These are removed by filling your subconscious with the truths of God, thereby cleansing the deeper mind in Divine order.

The fast spoken of in the Bible means to refrain from thinking of ideas and concepts which do not conform to the eternal verities. Fast from all thoughts, ideas, and beliefs that are not in the beam of God's broadcasting.

Learn to fast from the poisoned feast of the world. Real fasting is psychological, as when you turn your attention away from false suggestions and erroneous concepts of God, and, instead, feast on the eternal truths which heal, bless, and dignify your soul. Become a real pioneer and travel new roads by your spiritual thinking and imaging in the field of your own mentality.

CLOTHING THE NAKED

IS IT NOT to deal thy bread to the hungry, and that thou bring the poor that are cast out to thy house? when thou seest the naked, that thou cover him . . . ? (Isaiah 58:7).

The hungry and poor represent your hopes, desires, ideals, plans, and purposes still unrealized. These come to the temple of your own mind for acceptance and realization. Whatever is accepted by your mind comes into your experience. Let your mind be a temple beautiful, before which your ideals will be fed and clothed with faith and confidence.

The "naked" represent your ideals which are not yet nourished nor acted upon. Become emotionally attached to your ideal, and it will come to pass. Whatever you mentally and emotionally unite with comes to pass in Divine order.

And the Lord . . . shall make fat thy bones: and thou shalt be like a watered garden . . . (Isaiah 58:11). The bones represent the structure in your mind—the mental picture. It must be clothed with flesh and made alive. In other words, you must take that idea (which is the bone) into your mind and feel the reality of it. Symbolically, bones maintain the structure of your body and give you support.

Likewise, the plan, idea, or desire in your mind, when clothed with faith, assurance, and confidence, will be deposited in your subconscious mind and come to pass. You need to be fed mentally and spiritually as well as physically. Recognize your Higher Self and realize your oneness with It.

HEALTH SPRINGS FORTH SPEEDILY

Then shall thy light break forth as the morning, and thine health shall spring forth speedily: and thy righteousness shall go before thee; the glory of the Lord shall be thy reward (Isaiah 58:8).

This is a very important paragraph and is of profound significance to all students of scientific prayer. After you have fasted from negative thoughts and have called on the Infinite Healing Presence for wholeness, beauty, and perfection, your health should spring forth speedily. When it does not, you should do the next best thing: Go to a physician, dentist, osteopath, or chiropractor as the condition demands. It is foolish to wait and let the malady get worse.

Remember, if you can't grow a tooth, it is best to go to a dentist and bless him. If you can't dissolve that growth or tumor speedily, go at once to a surgeon and bless him. He is God's man, also. All healing is spiritual, for the single reason that there is only One Healing Presence. . . . *I am the Lord that healeth thee* (Exodus 15:26).

If you can precipitate yourself spiritually to New York City from Laguna Hills, you won't need a plane, automobile, or horse, or any other means of conveyance. However, rather than walking the distance, I suggest you go by plane or train if one is available. This does not mean, however, that if you were at a high level of consciousness you could not go from

Laguna Hills to New York City without any objective means of conveyance.

If you could dematerialize your body and cause the electrons to coalesce and precipitate in New York City—fine. Then you won't need any transportation. Some men down through the ages have been able to appear and disappear at will. You are told that Jesus disappeared in the multitude.

Your body is not solid. It is composed of waves of light. One scientist recently remarked that it is composed of octillion number of atoms, which is beyond my imagination. Octillion represents one (1) followed by eighteen zeroes.

LEVELS OF FAITH

If you can't dissolve a tumor in the breast or creative organs, and if it does not disappear speedily after prayer, this means you have not reached the level of faith necessary to do so. This is why you do the next best thing immediately. If you can staunch bleeding from an arterial wound—wonderful! You won't need any assistance. If you can't stop bleeding by prayer, you had better apply a tourniquet temporarily until you reach a doctor or hospital.

If you can save a child from drowning by speaking the word for her—wonderful! Otherwise, in an emergency it is best to dive in with all your clothes on and rescue the child. If you had the absolute faith, the child would be lifted out of the water and it would not be necessary for you to jump into the water to effect a rescue.

A longing for faith is not faith. Affirming, "God is healing me now" will not necessarily get results if there is a subconscious fear of the disease or a belief of incurability. All such fear has to be eradicated from the mind. Act according to the level of your consciousness or faith. You can always grow in your awareness in the same manner as you can grow in your faith in mathematics, chemistry, or any other principle of life.

THE MASS MIND OR LAW OF AVERAGES

Remember, if you were always walking in the consciousness of God's love and peace, you would be immune to all harm, disease, and trouble. All of us are in the mass mind. No matter how vigilant we are, some of these negative vibrations enter in. These are the tares mentioned in the Bible that grow up with the wheat. The tares represent the negative thoughts, fears, and false beliefs ,of the mass mind which enter our mind when we are not vigilant and are off guard.

This is why we have to be constantly on the *qui vive* and keep prayed up; then there will be no room in our mind for these negative subjective emanations coming from four billion people in the world. Subconsciously we are all one and are telepathically communicating all the time. This is why you are told to dwell in the secret place and abide in the shadow of the Almighty. *There shall no evil befall thee, neither shall any plague come nigh thy dwelling* (Psalm 91:10).

GROWING IN FAITH

As we continue to practice the Presence of God, we will grow in faith and understanding. Gradually we will secure a working conviction of God's Presence so that when we say, . . . *Stretch forth thine hand* . . . (Matthew 12:13), it is done according to "the word."

Let your affirmations of truth be a convincing demonstration of Spirit. You prove your faith by operating the laws of mind and getting results. The tangible results establish you in the knowledge of the truth, which sets you free.

Then shall thy light break forth as the morning, and thine health shall spring forth speedily . . . (Isaiah 58:8). *Behold, the Lord's hand is not shortened, that it cannot save; neither his ear heavy, that it cannot hear* (Isaiah 59:1).

Man is prone to disbelieve this possibility. He cannot quite believe the wonders of God, saying: "Well, yes, but, after all, we live in a physical body; and if I were born with a short arm, I can't do anything about it." At the same time he gives only lip service to: . . . *With God all things are possible* (Mark 10:27).

The late and famous Harry Edwards, the great healer in England, through the laying on of hands, has performed marvelous healings, straightening out legs and arms and healing all manner of diseases. He was a layman, but he believed that with God all things were possible.

They hatch cockatrice' eggs, and weave the spider's web: he that eateth of their eggs dieth . . . (Isaiah 59:5). The conflict of beliefs is here described graphically. Resistances to healings and to

the good things of life seem to rule and hold sway as iniquities, which is the meaning of "weaving of spider's web."

Millions today are psychologically overstimulated but going
nowhere spiritually. We find thousands of people following
various cults such as satanism, witchcraft, sorcery, voodoo, etc.,
referred to by Isaiah as "cockatrice's eggs."

There is a crying need for a mental and spiritual renais-
sance in order to escape the clouds of iniquities which beset
us. We need to find peace with the inner God Presence and
move onward and upward, and go from glory to glory.

10

Spiritual Powers You Can Apply

OUR PARTY ARRIVED in Honolulu and everyone was delighted to set foot on U. S. soil again. It was the fifth and sixth visit to Hawaii for several on our tour. A circle tour of the Island of Oahu enables one to see some of the island's most scenic attractions, such as Sealife Park, one of the world's most extensive and colorful marine areas, and Pearl Harbor, which is most interesting and informative.

The most fascinating and colorful of all the islands is the big island of Hawaii. After a few days in Hawaii, we winged our way across the Pacific to San Francisco for a good night's rest before starting on our way back home. My home is 3242—2H San Amadeo, Laguna Hills, California 92653.

A SPIRITUAL MESSAGE

During my first week as a resident of Leisure World, a man came to see me, asking me to interpret a dream for him which he considered to be very important. For three consecutive nights he had what is called a recurrent dream, which is very important because it is actually saying to him, "Stop, look, and listen."

A man had appeared to him in his dream, saying, "This is the third time I am coming to you. In the mouth of two or three witnesses shall every word be established." These words are from II Corinthians 13:1. *Examine yourselves, whether ye be in the faith; prove your own selves. Know ye not your own selves, how that Jesus Christ is in you, except ye be reprobates?* (II Corinthians 13:5). . . . *Be perfect, be of good comfort, be of one mind, live in peace; and the God of love and peace shall be with you* (II Corinthians 13:11).

This man was a student of the Bible, and his subconscious responded to his problem in the form of verses from Corinthians, which had a profound significance for him. In the correct esoteric or hidden understanding of the Bible, it must be understood that principles are personified as persons in order to make portrayal and interaction vivid and forceful.

The meaning of the third visit spoken of by Paul and the two or three witnesses can only be explained when we understand that persons, names, places, journeys, and events are symbols of changes in our mind. "Paul" means "the little Christ," or man awakening to the Power of God within him. He comes in three visits and is telling this man what to do. The first visit is a conception or desire, an idea in his mind. He had perfected an invention which he was trying to promote, and he had received some rejections by several local companies and industries. He was doubtful about the eventual outcome and had a deep-seated fear of rejection.

I explained that the first step was to realize that his idea was good and to give it attention, realizing that the Infinite Presence which gave him the idea would also reveal the perfect plan for its unfoldment. Further, he was to imagine his wife congratulating him every night prior to sleep on the acceptance of his invention. To be precise, he was to imagine the happy ending, the Divine solution. One of the best techniques was for him to get into a drowsy, sleepy state, which brings an outcropping of the subconscious mind, then hear his wife congratulating him on the acceptance of his invention.

In this subjective, passive state, he is actually impregnating his subconscious mind. As he repeats the process, the idea gradually sinks into his subconscious and becomes a conviction. Results then inevitably follow. This is the stage of the second witness wherein you begin to feel the possible fruition of your desire.

The third visit: The third witness is still to come, which means the outward manifestation following a sense of inner conviction of victory.

This explanation satisfied him. After about a week, he met a Japanese scientist at a social gathering who was connected with a large organization. Arrangements were made to purchase his invention and give him royalties, all of which were satisfactory to him.

THE INNER MEANING OF JESUS CHRIST

Paul says: *Know ye not . . . that Jesus Christ is in you, except ye be reprobates?* (II Corinthians 13:5). The inner meaning is this: One of the meanings of Jesus or Joshua is I AM, Je Suis. The inner meaning of Christ is the Presence of God in you. Symbolically speaking, all Paul is saying is that Jesus Christ means that your own I AMness is the Presence and Power of God in you. Psychologically speaking, you are Jesus Christ in action when your conscious and subconscious mind synchronize and agree on the eternal verities of life. Your prayer is always answered when there is no longer any argument in your brain and heart. When your brain and heart agree and unite in concord, the married pair bring forth the joy of the answered prayer.

You are then no longer "reprobate," because you know that the solution to all problems is within you. From now on you recognize no other power but the Living Spirit Almighty within you, Which knows only the answer. Jesus (illumined conscious mind) puts on the Christ (wisdom of the subconscious) and, fully integrated, becomes Jesus Christ—the ideal man!

ALIGN YOURSELF WITH THE INFINITE

A little boy once exasperated his father by putting together a completely cut up world map in a few minutes instead of taking a peaceful, quiet hour planned by his parents. Asked how he had succeeded so quickly in putting the world together, the boy said: "Why, Father, I simply put the man together on the other side of the map picture." The moral is: Let man unite with the God-Self and become integrated by his sense of oneness with the Divinity which shapes our ends.

Learn to Condition Yourself Spiritually

Begin to think, speak, and act from the Divine Center and not from the superimposed structure of fear, ignorance, and superstition. Affirm constantly: "God thinks, speaks, acts, and reacts through me." Think and speak from the standpoint of the principles of harmony, health, peace, joy, love, beauty, and right action. If you are a professor of mathematics, you think and speak from the standpoint of the principles of mathematics; likewise, begin to speak and act from the standpoint of the principles of life, which are the same yesterday, today, and forever.

Learn to condition yourself to the truths of God alone as they resound in the silence of your soul, so that you will not be frightened by the din, noise, and propaganda of the world but will follow the tones of the bugle of the Spirit. This will assure you of victory over the negations of the world.

The Arabian Horses

Recently I heard a trainer speak of the manner in which horses are trained to react to the sound of bugles, which are the sole means used in their training to response commands. They are given no food or water for four and one-half days, after which responses are called forth by bugle tones alone in various situations. This is a conditioning process which works.

Likewise, we must abstain from the food of the world representing the propaganda of fear, sickness, war, and prognostications and predictions of catastrophes. We must drink of the waters of life, such as inspiration, love, joy, laughter, and a transfusion of confidence and faith in the goodness of God in the land of the living.

WHAT IS EDUCATION?

The word "education" means to draw forth the wisdom, intelligence, and powers from our subjective depths, which will enable us to lead a full, happy, and coordinated life. I have talked with a number of college students who have acquired a large mass of facts, but their personal lives were chaotic. What they had learned seemed to have no relationship to their daily activities and expression in life.

Education should build character and morality. Knowledge is important, but it must be used wisely. The factor that makes for success in the art of living—for vitality and achievement—is not mere knowledge, but inspiration, wisdom, enthusiasm, cordiality, and goodwill. The so-called progressive education is completely wrong in its declaration that you must not learn how to curb certain urges and instincts which are negative in character growth and social existence.

The young boy or girl must be trained in correct inhibition. The world is full of educated derelicts. You find many of them in the skid rows of the world. Their negative and destructive thinking brought them there. They had made very poor mental investments.

A few nights ago there appeared on TV a young man eighteen years of age who had graduated from high school in New York City. He admitted to the interrogators that he could not even read what the diploma said. His parents apparently were suing the Board of Education for damages.

Wisdom Is Within You

While talking with an elderly man in the Hilton Hotel in Honolulu, he showed me a forked hazel stick which he uses to find water in places where people say there is no water. He has a natural wisdom and believes that the intelligence in his subconscious will guide him to the exact spot.

He pointed out that his father and grandfather were dowsers, the term applied to people possessing that skill, and were extraordinarily successful in finding oil, water, and minerals. They were ofttimes employed by some of the largest corporations.

This belief was communicated to him when a boy by his father and grandfather, and he accepted completely what they said. His subconscious responded accordingly. He stated he could tell by "its pull" toward a spot in the ground where water could be found, no matter how arid and unlikely a place it seemed to the senses. It had proved true in nearly all his experiences, he indicated.

He did not think it strange for the hazel stick to act this way. He knew there was no power in the hazel stick, as it was only a technique of tapping the subconscious. The wisdom of his subconscious acted upon the hazel stick, which revealed the answer to him. He could also tell how many feet to dig before water would be found. One time it was twenty feet, and the geologists confirmed it exactly.

The wisdom of the ages is hidden in your subjective depths.

Begin to tap the deep reservoirs within you, using the tools of faith and confidence. Wonders will happen in your life.

His Name Is Wonderful

Recently I talked with a widow in Reno, Nevada, who told me something very interesting. She said that everything had been going wrong in her life—finances in disarray, turmoil in her home, family problems, etc. She sat down one day in her dining room, however, and affirmed for about a half an hour: "It is wonderful." She did not ask herself, "What is wonderful?" To her the affirmation meant that God would work wonders in all phases of her life and that the word "wonderful" included all the things she desired in her heart.

She practiced this one-half hour meditative technique three times a day. On the third day she had an intense desire to play in the casino, where she won a large sum of money. She was able to pay all her bills and still had a considerable sum left for investment. Her winning attracted attention, and she fell in love with one of her admirers—a professional man. Everything in her life was transformed.

"It is wonderful" includes all things you could desire. . . . *and his name shall be called Wonderful, Counsellor, The mighty God, The everlasting Father, The Prince of Peace* (Isaiah 9:6).

He Wanted to Write

A school teacher told me recently that be began to mentally act as though publishers were hungry for his writings, since many of his submitted manuscripts had been returned to him apparently unread. He began to assume that he had letters of acceptance from several publishers.

He continued this imaginary drama for ten or fifteen minutes every night for about two weeks. One morning he had an intense desire to write something new and quite original. On its completion, he sent it off to one of the publishers who had previously rejected his writings, and it was accepted with *éclat*. As he assumed he had the necessary talent, his subconscious gave him the necessary ability and material enabling him to flower as a writer. He knew that the willingness of the publisher to accept his writings was proof of his inner ability to create.

How He Won Promotion

A young salesman who had been reading one of my books, *The Power of Your Subconscious Mind,** said that every night he would get still and bring about physical immobility bordering on the sleepy state. He would then imagine he was in front of his boss, who was congratulating him on work well done and telling him that he was now being promoted. He felt the genuineness of all this, so much so that it had all the vividness and distinctness of reality. He made the desired occurrence take place in his mind now. There was the imaginary handshake plus the animated conversation associated with it.

---

* See *The Power of Your Subconscious Mind* by Dr. Joseph Murphy, Prentice-Hall, Inc., Englewood Cliffs, N.J., 1963.

He knew that the drama of his mind was taking place subjectively and would have to be objectified sooner or later. He did not visualize himself at a distance in some point of space or some future time. On the contrary, he dramatized the whole thing as taking place now. Remember, the future event is a reality now at higher levels of your mind. You do not see yourself as though you were on a motion picture screen; on the contrary, you feel yourself in action here and now. He imagined his superior right in front of him and felt the reality of the imaginary handshake. This is the road to success.

HOW TO PRAY FOR ANOTHER

If another asks you to pray for him, be it a belief in sickness, poverty, or any other problem, you must loose the condition from your mind and let it go, not by using words of denial, but by claiming and believing that he is now experiencing what he longs to be and that he now possesses what he longs to possess. In other words, you picture him in your mind as he ought to be, while knowing that the action of God is taking place in his life.

In that way you forgive him. You change your concept of him. Complete forgetfulness is forgiveness. If you do not forget his ailment and problem, you have not forgiven. You forgive when you forget. If you see a person or think of him and you are reminded of what you had against him, you have not forgiven at all. Forgiveness is forgetfulness.

You Can't Give God Anything

The idea of "sacrifice" is based upon giving something up to God (your Higher Self). God is all there is, in all and over all, through all and all in all, and possesses all already. Why would man sacrifice lambs, bullocks, doves, etc., as if God were a cannibalistic Moloch who must be appeased? Some try to bargain with God, saying: "If God will heal my son, I will give up drinking."

All this is absolute nonsense. God is the Impersonal Presence and Power animating all things and is no respecter of persons. This sacrificial idea is a hangover from jungle days when primitive people tried to appease God by sacrificing animals and even children.

You cannot give God (I AM in you) anything but recognition, praise, and thanksgiving. What you sacrifice or give up is your false beliefs, fears, doubts, and other negative concepts. Read the 100th Psalm. Then you will have the right approach to the Infinite. For example, many people who want a healing imagine they are talking to their Higher Self and affirm: "Thank you, Father, for my miraculous healing." They repeat this silently over and over again until they enter into the mood of thankfulness. As they continue, they rise high enough in consciousness to the point of acceptance, and their subconscious mind responds to their belief. Every man answers his own prayer.

PRACTICING BY THE BOOK

There is quite a difference between a practitioner operating under grace and one who simply goes by the book. It is the consciousness of love that heals and restores the soul. There are not very many practitioners who work like Phineas Quimby in 1847, who took on all challenges and all manner of diseases without hesitation.

He was able to stop in its tracks the thing which his quaking patients feared would come upon them. He banished the idea of a punitive God from the minds of people and clairvoyantly perceived the root cause of their maladies. He operated from a high level of God consciousness. He brought about an electronic induction of grace, faith, and courage in his patients, who reported blessings, healings, and many gifts of the Spirit. Whether we are dealing with the medical, psychological, or spiritual healer, there is always room at the top.

THE TWO SCIENTISTS

One of our laboratory scientists said that science did not need a God, since he could reduce man to a mass of chemicals and water worth about $1.50 in today's market and place the contents in a large test tube. A Chinese chemist retorted, however, saying that only God could take the man out of the test tube and put him together again in one piece. This was rather a good rejoinder.

WHAT GARMENT DO YOU WEAR?

You are told in the 100th Psalm: *Serve the Lord with gladness: come before his presence with singing . . . into his courts with praise: be thankful unto him and bless his name* (Psalm 100:2,4).

The garment you wear when you pray must be one of confidence, praise, and thanksgiving. That is the proper mood, or garment. You must be receptive, open-minded, and ready to receive all the blessings which were given to you from the foundation of time. "All things be ready if the mind be so."

Every night of your life as you go to sleep, you are going before the King of Kings, the Lord of Lords, the Living Spirit Almighty, the God-Presence within you. If you go before a human king as a servant, you will get the duties of the servant or slave, as the case may be. If you go before the king of some country wearing the bars of a general, you will get an appropriate assignment.

For example, if you are called before some very prominent person, you will wear your most expensive clothes. You will not be very particular whether your suit is pressed or your tie is in order before the maid or servant, but if you are going before the President of the United States, you will be very conscious of your dress.

You visit the King of Kings, spiritually speaking, every night as you go off into the deep of sleep. Wear the garment of love, peace, goodwill, and expectancy. You wear the garment of faith in the fact that the nature of Infinite Intelligence responds when you call upon It. Never go to sleep wearing a garment of depression, anger, resentment, or self-condemnation. Then your garment is full of holes, seams, dirty and ragged at the edges. Inasmuch as the subconscious always magnifies what you deposit in it, you are generating more trouble.

Cleanse your mind prior to sleep. Forgive yourself and everybody else, and go to God with a song of praise in your heart. God will pour you out a blessing so bountiful there will not be room enough to receive it. Your last waking concept is engraved in your subconscious mind, the book of life, and records everything you feel and believe.

God is absolute love and grants whatever you claim and feel to be true. God is impersonal. *For the Lord is good; his mercy is everlasting; and his truth endureth to all generations* (Psalm 100:5).

11

The Answer Is Within You

A WOMAN SAID that she wanted to become thin. She was imitating the habits of others, who follow their diets with no results. All the time she was repressing in her subconscious her desire for apple pie, ice cream, and cookies. Her experiments were followed by an increase in weight later.

I pointed out to her that it was no use imitating the habits of others and that all she had to do was to decide on the weight desired (such as 120 pounds), and then claim: "I weigh 120 pounds in Divine law and order," repeating the statement many times a day, especially prior to sleep. I explained that as she continued to do this, the idea of 120 pounds would be conveyed to her subconscious mind, which would automatically cause her to lose all desire for foods which contributed to her adiposity.

SHE ESTABLISHED A CONSTRUCTIVE HABIT

Many times during the day, whether ironing clothes, washing the dishes, or using the vacuum, she would sing out loud to herself: "I weigh 120 pounds in Divine law and order. It is wonderful!" She repeated this conscious choice over and over again until it became habitual and entered into her subconscious mind. She knew that by repeating a certain thought, and feeling the joy and wonder of it all, it would find its way in due time into the subconscious and become law.

After a week or so she lost all desire for the amylaceous foods which were the cause of her obesity. When she used the words, "It is wonderful," it meant to her that God was working wonders in her life. . . . *And his name shall be called Wonderful . . .* (Isaiah 9:6).

HE PROMOTED HIMSELF

A young banker told me that every night he relaxed in a chair, closed his eyes, and focussed his attention on the president of his company. In his imagination he experienced the president congratulating him on his promotion and excellent work. He participated in the imaginary action of shaking hands with the president and hearing his voice, making it as real as possible. He lived the role with all the vividness and distinctness of reality. He did not see himself at a distance being congratulated. He made there here and the future now. He made it all so real that oftentimes when he opened his eyes he was amazed that the president was not physically present.

After a month's visualization and repetition of the mental movie, he succeeded in impregnating his subconscious mind and promotion followed in due course. He was also sent at the bank's expense to a special class in banking and was later made vice president.

The Thing He Greatly Feared

Job said, . . . *The thing which I greatly feared is come upon me . . .* (Job 3:25). Recently I talked with a man who had just begun learning the laws of mind. He said that for three years he had experienced a constant fear that his store would be held up by gunmen, and then it finally happened. He said that had he known the laws of mind, he would have reversed it and realized that *which I greatly love is come upon me*. He realized that he was dealing with the power that moves the world and was using it erroneously. All the power of the God-Presence is within the subconscious mind.

He now knows that he attracted the robbery to himself. He perceives now that nothing comes into our experience unless the equivalent is in our consciousness. Consciousness means your total beliefs and acceptances, both conscious and subconscious. In other words, it is the sum total of what you think, feel, believe, and give mental consent to. What is not in our consciousness we cannot experience.

He has begun now to make a habit of reading, believing, and

announcing the truths of the 91st Psalm to his subconscious mind several times a day. These eternal verities will enter his subconscious and become effective and functional in his life. His mind is now at peace and his abnormal fear has vanished.

LIKE ATTRACTS LIKE

What you really feel as true about yourself deep down in your heart will be verified on the screen of space. The great truth is that as a man thinketh in his heart (that is, emotionally and subconsciously), so does he act, experience, and function in life.

A detective who attends my lectures in Laguna Hills told me of a woman who had shaped her own attack. She had been attacked and raped. In her purse he found clippings of cases of rape going back several years. She told the detective that she knew it would happen to her. The detective referred to her as a victim in search of a rapist. Whatever we plant—good or bad—in our subconscious, we experience sooner or later.

WHY HE FAILED

During a consultation with a young businessman, I learned that he worked very hard, was industrious, forthright, and progressive in his thought and general attitude; however, he had suffered repeated failures due to the fact that he felt a jinx was following him, that he could not succeed, that fate was against him, and that somehow he was not destined to succeed.

I explained to him that he was born to win and destined to succeed because the Infinite Presence and Power within him was Omnipotent and was always successful in all Its undertakings, whether creating new stars or making a tree. He realized that he was making a law for himself because of the repeated suggestions he gave to his subconscious, which in turn responded to his belief in failure.

He now understands that whatever we believe in, the subconscious brings to pass. He made a new law for himself and began to reiterate the idea of success and wealth, knowing that by constant repetition of those two ideas and by living the role in his mind, picturing his wife congratulating him on his success and wealth, these two ideas would eventually become deposited in his subconscious. The law of the subconscious being compulsive, he would, therefore, be compelled to succeed and become wealthy.

In a month's time his whole life changed due to the new good habit established in his subconscious mind. Prayer is a good habit; failure is a bad habit. He discovered that his thought-image and feeling transformed his life. He also made sure that while he was reprogramming his subconscious mind, he did not deny what he had previously affirmed.

THE POWER TO CHOOSE

The Bible says: . . . *Choose you this day whom ye will serve* . . . (Joshua 24:15). While conversing with a foreign intelligence officer in India, he revealed the hazards to which he was exposed almost every day. He said that in studying the Bhagavad Gita and the Psalms in the Bible, he discovered there was but One Power, which was absolutely good and perfect.

He added that all he had to do was to sell himself completely on the protective power of God—the Only One. Every morning and every evening he read aloud these verses from the 27th Psalm: *The Lord is my light and my salvation; whom shall I fear? the Lord is the strength of my life; of whom shall I be afraid? . . . For in the time of trouble he shall hide me in his pavilion: in the secret of his tabernacle shall he hide me; he shall set me up upon a rock* (Psalm 27:1,5).

He repeated these truths over and over again every morning before going out on an assignment. He constantly reminded himself of these verses during the day. He knew that by constantly repeating these marvelous truths with his conscious mind, they would gradually penetrate his subconscious mind, which is reactive to the mental patterns impressed upon it. He also knew that he was establishing a beneficent habit and that the result would be an automatic response from his deeper mind, resulting in the fact that he would lead a charmed life.

This is what has happened. In one instance, for example, a man fired point blank at him and the gun jammed. In another instance, a man threw a bomb at him in his car and it failed to explode. In another instance, an inner voice spoke clearly to him informing him the food he was about to eat was poisoned. He did not touch it.

Emerson says, "There is guidance for each of us, and by lowly listening we shall hear the right word." He calls this inner voice which speaks to him the voice of "Om" or "I AM," which, in our Bible, means the Presence of God, the Higher Self or the Superconscious. All these names mean the same thing. The Divine Presence is lodged in the subconscious of everyone, which Emerson called the "Oversoul."

When you repeat a certain thought over and over again in a meaningful way, the moment comes when it becomes a realization—a subconscious conviction resulting in the automatic response of your deeper mind, which guides, directs, and propels you to green pastures and still waters.

FALSE BELIEF

A school teacher had been told that the reason his ailing leg would not heal was due to the fact that he was now paying off a karmic penalty for misdeeds in a former life. He was a principal in a school and obviously well-educated from an academic standpoint.

I explained to him that all this was imaginative folderol and an insult to his native intelligence. Furthermore, I suggested that he go to two reputable professors of psychology and have them regress him to the same period of time, which was, according to his reading, one hundred years before his birth. He had readings from both men separately. They did not know each other; each reading was a complete contradiction of the other. In one instance, one hundred years before his birth he was a woman in Kentucky who had four children. The other reading for the same period of time revealed that he was a soldier in France and had been imprisoned for shooting his commanding officer.

It is obvious that these readings of his immediate past life (one hundred years prior to birth here) were fictionalized dramatizations of his subconscious and were purely imaginary. He spoke French fluently in the second reading, but he reads and understands French anyway. He was quite intrigued. He went to another psychologist for a third reading, which contradicted everything the two previous psychologists had recorded. He also asked the third psychologist to read his present life from the moment of birth. (He is fifty-five years of age.)

Everything is recorded in the subconscious mind; i.e., all his experiences from the cradle to the present moment are impressed indelibly and infallibly in the universal subconscious mind. Therefore, the material of his deeper mind should be accessible to these experts in life readings and regression under hypnosis. The result was a miserable failure to record events in his present life.

This teacher's eyes were opened. He declared, "I have been had," by which he meant he had been bamboozled by all this tomfoolery. I sent him to a physician, an old friend of mine, who told him he would have a perfect healing with the new medication he applied to the leg. This suggestion from the doctor was accepted by his subconscious mind and he was delighted.

It was his right leg which was afflicted. The right leg means the objective world, and legs mean motion. He admitted that he didn't want to be transferred from where he was and was fighting it in his mind. He was suffering from suppressed rage and resentment. These emotions, being negative, had to have an outlet; so his subconscious responded with leg trouble. This is called organ language.

He decided to let go and let God guide and direct him. In other words, he surrendered the whole thing to the Infinite Presence and Power, using this prayer: "Infinite Intelligence guides the doctor to do the right thing. I surrender to the Infinite Intelligence, and I am Divinely led to do the right thing. I am always in my true place, doing what I love to do, Divinely happy, and Divinely prospered. God in the midst of me is healing me now and I give thanks for the miraculous healing taking place now."

His leg has been healed now and he is happy where he is. He decided to let go and let God take over. This attitude leads all of us to ways of pleasantness and to paths of peace.

She Was Hearing Voices

A woman who was using the Ouija Board came to see me and showed me some writings which she had received when she began using the Board, some of which were very good and full of Biblical verses and quotations. After a few weeks, she said a voice took over and every night this inner voice would shout obscenities at her, tell her to commit suicide or to get drunk, and it made lewd and evil remarks to her.

In using the Ouija Board, she was in constant fear that some so-called evil entity would enter in and, as Job said, . . . *The thing which I greatly feared is come upon me* . . . (Job 3:25).

In other words, her subconscious mind acted on her constant fear and responded in the above negative fashion.

I gave her a special prayer to use, one which I have sent out over the years to many people who believe they are controlled by some evil entities. Love casts out fear. The constant realization of the Presence of God animating you, sustaining you, guiding and directing you will dissolve and eradicate all negative forces.

Following is the prayer I gave her, with instructions to repeat it aloud for about ten minutes morning, afternoon, and prior to sleep at night, knowing that by the reiteration of these truths constantly to the subconscious mind, all negation and fear would be removed. She began to affirm these truths regularly and systematically, knowingly and feelingly, until they became a living part of her mentality.

THE SPECIAL PRAYER

"God loves me and cares for me. God's love fills my conscious and subconscious mind. I know that by affirming these truths I will dethrone from my mind all negative influences. I affirm these truths boldly. I mean every word, and what I decree comes to pass. God lives in me. God talks in me. God walks with me. My life is God's life, and God's peace fills my mind and heart. God's healing love saturates my whole being. Wisdom, truth, and beauty govern me. I am whole, I am happy, I am peaceful, and the joy of the Lord is my strength.

"Where God is there is no evil. I can do all things through the God Power Which strengtheneth me. I know whatever I attach to "I AM" I become. God careth for me. I am surrounded by the sacred circle of God's eternal love, and the whole armor of God enfolds me. His light shines in my mind. I hear the truth; I know the truth; I hear the still, small voice of God saying to me, 'Peace be still.' "

Following this meditation she issued the command boldly, incisively, and decisively: "I decree you get out now. I mean it. I decree it. Get thee hence. God is, and His love is here now. Be thou gone. I am free. Thank you, Father."

After a week or so, following this prayer technique, she was completely free, and she also ceased dabbling with the Ouija Board. She now knows it was her own subconscious mind talking back to her. In other words, she was talking to herself.

Born Again

Many people ask me the meaning of this statement. We read in the papers almost every day of someone claiming that he is born again. This has nothing to do with physical birth, however. You might be a great mathematician or an outstanding physician, but this is not spiritual enlightenment or illumination. Man must be aware of spiritual powers within him and have a sense of oneness with the Infinite. In other words, when Divine love and Divine peace fill his soul and when he begins to think, speak, and act from the Divine Center within him, then he experiences what is called a spiritual rebirth and is completely free from fear, ignorance, superstition, and false beliefs of the world.

He has no denominational religion, neither does he belong to any sectarian creed, because he knows intuitively that God is no respecter of persons, and that you cannot put a label on love, peace, harmony, joy, goodwill, inspiration, or right action.

REBIRTH CAN TAKE PLACE NOW

Rebirth is an individual experience. . . . *Except a man be born of water and of the Spirit, he cannot enter into the kingdom of God* (John 3:5). Water is your mind, which, like water, will take the shape of any vessel into which it is poured. Fill your mind with the truths of God morning, noon, and night, and as you saturate your subconscious with the eternal verities, your whole life will be transformed into the image and likeness of your contemplation.

"All things be ready if the mind be so" (Shakespeare). You can open your heart now to the influx of the Holy Spirit and be renewed and illumined from On High.

HE SAID, "IN TIME ALL WILL BE BORN AGAIN"

A young clergyman with whom I was well acquainted had the illusion that in time everybody here in the world would experience a spiritual rebirth. I referred him to the Third Chapter of Ecclesiastes:

To every thing there is a season, and a time to every purpose under the heaven:

A time to be born, and a time to die; a time to plant, and a time to pluck up that which is planted;

A time to kill, and a time to heal; a time to break down, and a time to build up;

A time to weep, and a time to laugh; a time to mourn, and a time to dance;

A time to cast away stones, and a time to gather stones together; a time to embrace, and a time to refrain from embracing;

A time to get, and a time to lose; a time to keep, and a time to cast away;

A time to rend, and a time to sew; a time to keep silence, and a time to speak;

A time to love, and a time to hate; a time of war, and a time of peace.

What profit hath he that worketh in that wherein he laboureth?

I have seen the travail, which God hath given to the sons of men to be exercised in it.

He hath made every thing beautiful in his time: also he hath set the world in their heart, so that no man can find out the work that God maketh from the beginning to the end.

I know that there is no good in them, but for a man to rejoice, and to do good in his life.

And also that every man should eat and drink, and enjoy the good of all his labour, it is the gift of God.

I know that, whatsoever God doeth, it shall be for ever: nothing can be put to it, nor any thing taken from it: and God doeth it, that men should fear before him.

That which hath been is now; and that which is to be hath already been; and God requireth that which is past (Ecclesiastes 3:1–15).

It is foolish to think that in time people will become God-like and saintly. This is an illusion. There is nothing wrong with the world or the galaxies in space. All are controlled by a Supreme Intelligence working mathematically, in an orderly manner, and with Infinite precision. It is said that order is heaven's first law.

It is the people in the world who must change, and it is an individual process. No one can wave a mystic wand and convert people to practice goodness, truth, and beauty. This world of ours revolves on its axis regularly and repeats the seasons regularly. All of us here in this three-dimensional world are moving through opposites—night and day, ebb and flow, sweet and sour, health and sickness, faith and fear, good and evil. We have to learn to reconcile the opposites and experience the peace that passeth understanding.

Our lives are like a pendulum, a sort of rhythmical alternation between its opposites. We move from war to peace; and, after an interval, go back to war again. This takes place because man is what he is. When greed, malice, hate, envy, and jealousy die out in man, then, of course, there will be no war, sickness, or crime.

This does not take place collectively; it takes place as each man learns to practice the Presence of God in his thoughts, in his words, and in his deeds. Each man creates his own utopia. No government can guarantee peace, happiness, health, or prosperity. There are countless thousands of people travelling around the world, and the writer has met many of them. Great numbers of them are familiar with the most remote areas, but they have not travelled within themselves where the Holy of Holies dwells—the Presence of God.

When you travel spiritually, you go up the Hill of God within yourself and contemplate the great truths of God. You then appropriate more and more of Divinity by meditation, prayer, and contemplation. There is no time or space in the Divine Presence within you, and your spiritual awakening has nothing to do with the time of the movement of the earth around the sun.

The Timeless, Spaceless, Ageless One is within you. You can be changed in the twinkling of an eye. *That which hath been is now; and that which is to be hath already been . . .* (Ecclesiastes 3:15).

History repeats itself, and that which was shall be again. This cycle of changes does not change America or the universe, but its aim and purpose is to change man so that he becomes the new man, the happy man, the joyous man, the man who has recognized God as his Father and all men as his brothers.

The universe is controlled by God. God works on the universal scale. Man is the particular, and in order for God to work through the particular, God must become the particular. This simply means that you are an individualization of God. In order for God to work through you, He can work only through your own thought patterns and imagery.

In verse 11 of this chapter, the inspired writer says: *He hath made every thing beautiful in his time: also he hath set the world in their heart . . .* The world you see is the world you are. You see through the contents of your own mentality. Beauty is in the eye of the beholder, and each one sees a different world. If your eyes are identified with that which is lovely and of good report, you will see only the lovely. "That thou seest man, that too become thou must. God if thou seest God, and dust if thou seest dust."

The travail spoken of in verse 10 means the various problems, challenges, trials, and difficulties we meet on the screen of space which enables us to grow spiritually by overcoming them. The great joy is in overcoming problems and in discovering the Power within you.

Cease trying to change the world. There is no one to change but yourself. Human nature has not changed much through the centuries, as is testified by the recent three great wars. Actually, war has been going on somewhere in the world ever since I was born. You have no magic wand to banish disease, which originates in the mind of man. Neither do you have that mystic stick that prevents war and human conflict.

This is a school, and we are here to learn to grow and discover the Divinity which shapes our ends. The suffering of the world, as Buddha said, is due to ignorance. It is noble and Godlike to desire to relieve the suffering and the sick, but you should not contemplate the crimes, tragedies, and suffering in the world to the point of depression. To do so is to pollute the mass mind some more. Contemplate peace, harmony, right action, and illumination for yourself and all mankind. You will then be giving a benediction to all mankind.

Take your good now. Take your happiness now. Take love now. Take joy now. Don't postpone your good. It is foolish to say that you will be happy, joyous, and free when wars cease and when all the people experience a rebirth in God—you will wait forever. When you walk in the consciousness of God's peace, harmony, and joy, you are blessing all people who walk the earth, because you are spreading to all the world the sunshine of His love.

We had a woman with us on our tour around the world who was overly sympathetic. Beggars flocked around her. Some wanted to grab her bag. She said, "I can't eat tonight thinking of all these poor hungry people." A fellow passenger spoke rather harshly to her, telling her to wake up. He said that the best thing she could do was to go and lie down with the beggars on the street and suffer with them. She saw the point. It does not help the hungry beggar to say, "I feel so sorry for you I have decided to starve with you." She could not possibly feed all the beggars who descended upon her; neither did she have enough money to buy all of them food and clothing.

When you visit a sick friend in the hospital, I am confident you don't say, "I am so sympathetic and so sorry for you. I have decided to stay here and suffer with you." What your sick friend really needs is a spiritual transfusion of faith, confidence, love, and goodwill. You can lift your sick friend up by reminding him of the healing power of God and of the miracles of healing taking place today everywhere. That is compassion—it is not sympathy.

In the Book of Matthew you have the answer: . . . *These ought ye to have done, and not to leave the other undone* (Matthew 23:23). To give a hungry man food is good, but you have not given him the other half. A little later he will be hungry again. Teach him how to tap his subconscious mind where the riches of heaven are. Let him know that God will supply all his needs, and when he calls God will answer him. Then you have given the other half—the pearl of great price—and he will never want again.

Remember the great truth: . . . *That every man should eat and drink, and enjoy the good of all his labour, it is the gift of God* (Ecclesiastes 3:13).

12

A Meditation on the 23rd Psalm

THE LORD IS *my shepherd; I shall not want.*

He maketh me to lie down in green pastures: he leadeth me beside the still waters.

He restoreth my soul: he leadeth me in the paths of righteousness for his name's sake.

Yea, though I walk through the valley of the shadow of death, I will fear no evil: for thou art with me; thy rod and thy staff they comfort me.

Thou preparest a table before me in the presence of mine enemies: thou anointest my head with oil; my cup runneth over.

Surely goodness and mercy shall follow me all the days of my life: and I will dwell in the house of the Lord for ever (Psalm 23:1–6).

Many people meditate on the great truths of this Psalm and get wonderful results. As you focus your attention on these truths, absorbing them into your mentality, you are meditating in the true sense of the word, because you are appropriating more of your Divinity—the God-Presence which dwells in your deep self.

The Lord is my shepherd. The Lord means God, the Living Spirit within you. *I shall not want.* This means you will never want for evidence of the fact that you have chosen God as your shepherd.

A shepherd watches over his sheep. He loves them and cares for them. He examines the fields where they graze, and he eradicates loco weed, which would adversely affect the sheep. He leads them to the shade and guides them single file over the steep ravine to water, where they are refreshed. At night he examines their nostrils to see if there are any needles or other irritants imbedded there. If so, he plucks them out and pours some soothing oil upon them. He examines their feet also and, if injured, administers kindly to them with whatever medication or treatment is appropriate.

The shepherd loves his sheep. He calls them by name and they follow him. All this is symbolic, of course, but very significant, indicating to all of us that if we choose God as our shepherd, we will not want for any good thing.

Verily, verily, I say unto you, He that entereth not by the door into the sheepfold, but climbeth up some other way, the same is a thief and a robber (John 10:1).

Before we get an answer to our prayer, we must first possess our desire in consciousness. Our consciousness represents the sum total of our acceptances and beliefs, both conscious and subconscious. Our state of consciousness is the way we think, feel, and believe, and to whatever we give mental consent.

In other words, our desire must be deposited in our subconscious mind. "I must be" before "I can have." The ancients said, "To be is to have." If I try to obtain what I want by external means, I am a thief and a robber. My state of consciousness is the door to all expression. I must possess the mental equivalent of whatever I want to be or possess.

Let us take a simple illustration. A person wants to be healed and affirms over and over, "I am healed." These mechanical statements are not enough. The person must enter into the joy and realization that he is healed. It must be a conviction based on the silent inner knowing of the soul. To be wealthy, man must assume the feeling of being wealthy; then wealth will follow.

The sheep are the noble, dignified, God-like ideas that bless us. Our conviction of good is the shepherd that watches over the sheep, because our dominant state of mind always rules, in the same manner as a general commands the army. We call our sheep by name when we enter into the consciousness of having, being, or doing the thing we long to have, to be, or to do. If we sustain these moods, they gel and crystallize within us, and these subjectified embodiments become objectified manifestation.

And a stranger will they not follow, but will flee from him: for they know not the voice of strangers (John 10:5). The strangers are the thoughts of fear, doubt, or anxiety which enter the mind. These ideas delay our healing and postpone our demonstration because these thoughts neutralize our good.

It is idle to pray that the Infinite Healing Presence is making you whole and perfect and at the same time be resentful or fearful that you cannot be healed. If you believe that circumstances, conditions, events, age, race, lack of money, etc. can preclude the possibility of attaining your objective, you are, in biblical language, a thief and a robber. This is why it is said, *All that ever came before me* (the conviction) *are thieves and robbers . . .* (John 10:8).

Meditation is for the purpose of redirecting your mind along God-like ways so that Divine law and order may govern all your activities and all phases of your life.

Shakespeare said, "All things be ready if the mind be so." The Bible says, . . . *The works were finished from the foundation of the world* (Hebrews 4:3). All this means is that we should open our minds and hearts and accept the gifts of God proffered to us from the foundation of time. We should reorder our minds and ask ourselves a simple question: How is it in God and Heaven? The answer is: All is bliss, harmony, joy, love, peace, perfection, wholeness, and indescribable beauty.

The All-Wise, the All-Powerful, and the All-Knowing One is within us. No matter what we seek already is. Love is, peace is, joy is, power is, harmony is, and the answer to every problem is within us now, at this moment. God knows only the answer.

HOW TO RECEIVE GUIDANCE

If you are seeking guidance, affirm: "Infinite Intelligence knows the answer, the way out, even before I ask. As I call on this Supreme Wisdom now, I know Its nature is to respond to me. I will clearly recognize the lead or answer when it comes. I know it comes clearly into my conscious, reasoning mind, and I recognize it instantaneously."

Having done this, dismiss it from your mind, knowing that you have turned your request over to the Infinite Intelligence in your subconscious and inevitably the answer will come. You know when you have really turned it over, because your mind is at peace, and you don't subsequently deny what you have already affirmed and decreed.

HE MAKETH ME TO LIE DOWN IN GREEN PASTURES

I am writing this chapter in Laguna Hills, California. A letter arrived in the mail yesterday from a woman in Hawaii telling me that she meditated on these words: *He maketh me to lie down in green pastures*, for about half an hour three times a day for a week. She focussed all her attention on this promise of the Psalm. She began to look at it from all angles, its inner meaning and how it applied to her.

She stated that in her meditative mood and on her reflection on these words, the phrase meant peace of mind, contentment, tranquility, abundance, and security. The vision of a cow lying down in the field chewing the cud came clearly into her mind, symbolizing the meditative process of her own mind. In chewing the cud, the cow is absorbing, digesting, and transforming everything eaten into milk, tissue, bone, muscle, blood, etc. Likewise, she was digesting, ingesting, and absorbing these truths until they too became a part of her.

Her finances were in bad shape. She was in danger of losing her lovely home. The mine in which she had invested a large part of her money suddenly collapsed. Her son was

missing—no one could find him. As she continued to meditate, at the end of the week she received notice from an attorney that a large sum of money had been bequeathed to her by
a distant relative on another island, as well as some stocks
and bonds. This solved her financial problem, and she was
able to make satisfactory arrangements with all concerned.
Her son returned home. He had run away to Canada, thinking there were green pastures there. He was wiser on his return and is at peace.

This was real meditation of a very constructive nature. She
appropriated mentally these great truths and they became a
living part of her in the same way that a banana, when eaten,
becomes a part of your bloodstream. She quietly devoted her
mind to a certain passage of the Psalm and dwelt on the pro-
fundity of its meaning and its healing power. She decided to
lie down mentally with these truths and experience all around
harmony in her life.

HE LEADETH ME BESIDE THE STILL WATERS

The shepherd in the Bible is a symbol of the guiding, healing,
protective power of the God-Presence within. You are a good
shepherd when you know and believe that God is the Only
Presence, Power, Cause, and Substance. When this conviction is enthroned in your mind, you will be Divinely directed
and blessed in countless ways.

The still waters represent the mind full of peace, poise, serenity, and equanimity. You are contemplating the power, the

wisdom, and the love of the Infinite. In doing so, you find yourself immersed in the Holy Omnipresence, bathed by the river of peace, joy, wholeness, and vitality. When your mind is at peace, the answer comes. Peace is the power at the heart of God.

. . . *To be spiritually minded is life and peace* (Romans 8:6).

HE RESTORETH MY SOUL

When you choose God as your shepherd, you will sing the song of triumph. Or, to put it in Emerson's words, your mental attitude is "the soliloquy of the loving and beholding soul." You are recognizing the Infinite Spirit within you, and you know there will be a response when you call upon It. Furthermore, you recognize the power as One and Indivisible. As you do this, you reject all the fears and false beliefs of the world.

Whatever fears, frustrations, and false beliefs were deposited in or became resident in your subconscious mind are now being obliterated and expunged, because you are claiming boldly that the Infinite ocean of life, love, truth, and beauty are saturating your subconscious, cleansing, healing, and transforming your whole being into the Divine patterns of harmony, wholeness, and peace. Once you acknowledge the supremacy of the One Healing Power and the creative power of your thought, you have the Lord, or God, as your shepherd and you have restored your soul.

Thou wilt keep him in perfect peace, whose mind is stayed on thee: because he trusteth in thee (Isaiah 26:3).

HE LEADETH ME IN THE PATHS OF RIGHTEOUSNESS FOR HIS NAME'S SAKE

Go within, close your eyes, become still and quiet, and gently affirm that the wisdom of God anoints your intellect and is always a lamp unto your feet and a light upon your path. Claim that Divine love goes before you making straight, happy, joyous, and prosperous your way. Look to the God-Presence at all times and think, speak, act, and react from the standpoint of the Divine Center within you.

Realize, know, feel, and claim that God is your guide, your counsellor, your boss, your senior partner, and that Divine right action governs you at all times. Affirm boldly: "From now on I think right because I think from the standpoint of eternal verities and principles of life. I feel right, I do right, I act right, and everything I do is in accordance with the eternal principle of Divine law and order—Heaven's first law. I know that the name of God means the nature of God, which refers to the fact that God is the Ever-Living One, the All-Powerful One, Infinite Intelligence, Omnipresent, Omniscient, and Boundless Love. I now know that God and His love saturate my whole being, and whatever I do will prosper."

YEA, THOUGH I WALK THROUGH THE VALLEY OF THE SHADOW OF DEATH, I WILL FEAR NO EVIL: FOR THOU ART WITH ME

Wherever you go, walk the earth with the consciousness of peace, love, and goodwill to all. Suppose you go into a hospital to see a sick friend and are taking with you the mood of love, peace, and goodwill. Your mental and spiritual atmosphere will bless the sick person. You are able to give a transfusion of grace and love to your friend, thereby nourishing him with faith, confidence, and a belief in the Infinite Healing Presence. God is life, and that is your life now.

God cannot die; therefore, there is no death. So-called death is an entry into the fourth dimension of life, and our journey is from glory to glory, from wisdom to wisdom, ever onward, upward, and Godward, for there is no end to the glory which is man.

The shadow means the nonreality of death. Every end is a beginning; therefore, when you leave this dimension, it will be your new birthday in God, and you will wear a new, fourth-dimensional body (which you have now), which is rarefied and attenuated, enabling you to pass through solid matter. You will meet your loved ones, and you will grow in wisdom, truth, and beauty there as well as here.

Actually, you go there every night when you go to sleep, when some men in their ignorance might call you dead. If, for example, you are afraid of death, of afterlife, or judgment day and things of that nature, then you are being governed by ignorance and delusion; not by the Lord of all, which is a God of love. *For God hath not given us the spirit of fear; but of power, and of love, and of a sound mind* (II Timothy 1:7). Death, in biblical language, is ignorance of the truths of God.

Thy Rod and Thy Staff They Comfort Me

The rod represents the power of God, which is instantly available to you when you call upon It. The staff represents your authority and ability to use It. To meditate and think about the Omnipotence and Omniscience of the Infinite Presence brings your mind to an inner state of quietude and passivity.

Think of a beautiful, quiet lake on a mountain top, which reflects the heavenly lights such as the stars and the moon. Likewise, when your mind is still and quiet, you will reflect the heavenly truths and lights of God. The quiet mind gets things done. When your mind is still, quiet, and receptive, the Divine idea or solution to your problem rises to your surface mind. That is the guidance and intuitive voice of the Infinite Presence and Power. When the lake on the mountain is disturbed, it does not reflect the lights of the heaven above.

Claim that God is guiding you now and give thanks for the joy of the answered prayer. His rod and staff have comforted you and you are at peace.

Thou Preparest a Table Before Me in the Presence of Mine Enemies

And a man's foes shall be they of his own household (Matthew 10:36). The enemies are your own thoughts, your fears, self-condemnation, doubts, anger, resentment, and ill will. The real enemies are always in your own mind. When fear thoughts come to your mind, supplant them with faith in God and all things good. When prone to engage in self-criticism or self-condemnation, supplant these thoughts immediately with this great truth: "I exalt God in the midst of me."

A young lady was making false allegations against her uncle, hoping to break a Will so she could get some of the money bequeathed to him. He was angry and was fighting the matter in his mind, making a nervous wreck of himself. However, when he saw what he was doing, he ceased fighting the matter in his mind and began to feed himself spiritually with the great truths of God. He contemplated peace, harmony, and Divine right action, and there was a Divine harmonious solution.

A medical doctor, a close friend of mine, said to me recently that the publicity given to the two wives of prominent politicians in Washington who had developed cancer of the breast caused a great fear, and numbers of women flocked to him for tests to see if they too had cancer. He added that he felt that fighting cancer, tuberculosis, heart disease, etc. through propaganda on the screen, radio, and press does more harm than good, because what we fight in our mind we magnify. He pointed out that the constant fear of cancer on the part of these women would ultimately create precisely the thing they fear. *For the thing which I greatly feared is come upon me . . .* (Job 3:25).

Walk in the consciousness of God's love, peace, wholeness, and perfection, and you will automatically rise above these false beliefs, fears, and propaganda by the mass mind. There is a prayer used in India by many people, which the young boy in a spiritually oriented family is taught: "I am all health. God is my health." As the young boy sings this to himself many times a day, it becomes a habit, and he gradually builds up an immunity to all sickness and disease.

Realize that there is nothing in God's universe to fear. Cease giving power to the created thing. Give power to the Creator. The whole universe is for you and nothing is against you.

THOU ANOINTEST MY HEAD WITH OIL

Oil is a symbol of light, healing, praise, and thanksgiving. This means that the Infinite Healing Presence is now functioning on your behalf, and the wisdom of God anoints your intellect. You are consecrated with Divine love. *Thou hast put gladness in my heart* . . . (Psalm 4:7). . . . *God hath anointed thee with the oil of gladness* . . . (Psalm 45:7). . . . *God hath anointed thee with the oil of gladness* . . . (Hebrews 1:9).

One of the most wonderful ways to get an answer to your prayer is to imagine you are addressing the Infinite in the silence of your soul. Lull yourself to sleep with the words, "Thank you, Father." Do this over and over again until you get the feeling of thankfulness. You are thanking the Infinite for the answer to your prayer. As you do this, you carry the thankful attitude to the deep of yourself, and wonders happen as you pray in this way.

MY CUP RUNNETH OVER

The cup is a symbol of your heart, which, by contemplation, you can fill with the great truths of God. As you contemplate the beauty, the glory, and the wonders of the Infinite, you will automatically generate a feeling of love, peace, and joy, which fills your heart with ecstasy and rapture. You will find yourself exuding vibrancy, cordiality, geniality, and good-will to all.

Your subconscious magnifies exceedingly what you deposit in it. Therefore, on introspection, you will find that your good is pressed down, shaken together, and running over with the fragrance of God. You will find that God's love has completely dissolved everything negative in your subconscious mind and that you are as free as the wind.

Surely Goodness and Mercy Shall Follow Me All the Days of My Life

As you continue to meditate and absorb these great truths of the 23rd Psalm, you will discover that all things are working together for your good. Divine love goes before you making happy and joyous your way. The harmony, peace, and joy of the Lord flow into your life and you find yourself expressing your talents at the highest possible level. You will discover that you become what you contemplate. When meditating on the truths of God, you will find that all your ways are pleasantness and all your paths are peace.

I Will Dwell in the House of the Lord Forever

You are the temple of the Living God. God indwells you and walks and talks in you. You dwell in the house, which is your own mind, when you regularly, systematically remind yourself many times a day that God is your guide, your counsellor, and that you are being constantly inspired from On High.

You look upon God as your Father, your Source of supply, and you know that you will never want for any good thing, because He loves you and cares for you. . . . *The tabernacle of God is with men, and he will dwell with them, and they shall be his people, and God himself shall be with them, and be their God* (Revelation 21:3).

You are now rooted to the Divine Presence and you are at home with God. He gives you rest and security. You are relaxed and at ease and completely free from fear, for where you are God is, and you dwell with God forever. You are on a journey up the celestial ladder that knows no end. Every night of your life, you go to sleep with the praise of God forever on your lips.

13

What Is Your Problem?

THE BIBLE SAYS: *Be still, and know that I am God...* (Psalm 46:10). What a wonderful release comes to your mind when you whisper these words to yourself in the silence of your soul. What a release of pressure, anxiety, and tension comes to you also when you dwell on the wisdom, truth, and beauty of the following great truth: ... *Stand ye still, and see the salvation of the Lord ...* (II Chronicles 20:17). *The Lord will perfect that which concerneth me ...* (Psalm 138:8).

When you saturate your mind with these truths, there will be a definite response from the Infinite Intelligence which indwells you and walks and talks with you.

HE SAID HE HAD TRIED EVERYTHING

A man living here in Laguna Hills had a difficult legal problem which had continued for nearly five years. He tried releasing it; he prayed about it and affirmed every night: "I let go and I let God take over." However, he was in the habit of negating his prayer during the day because he would "pick" at the situation, so to speak, every day, more or less saying, "How long, O Lord; how long?"

In our conversation he quoted a very familiar phrase from the Bible: *In the world ye shall have tribulation: but be of good cheer; I have overcome the world* (John 16:33). He had the idea that somehow he was being punished, since the lawsuit in which he was involved was based on false allegations and a tissue of lies on the part of relatives suing him over a Will. In other words, the plaintiffs were greedy and wanted something for nothing.

Following my advice, however, he came to an adjustment within himself and instead of fussing, fretting, and fuming during the day, he frequently affirmed: "I loose it and I let it go. It is God in action, which means all-around harmony and peace." This was a discipline of substitution. When the negative thoughts came to his mind, he would immediately supplant them with the above-mentioned affirmation. After several days these negative thoughts lost all momentum and he felt an inner sense of peace.

He ceased giving his relatives any power to hurt him or deprive him of his good, a power which they never had except in his own thought. Gradually he grew in spiritual awareness and understanding and impregnated himself with the conviction that his own consciousness was the only cause of his experiences and conditions in life. By consciousness he meant the sum total of his conscious and subconscious acceptances and beliefs. As Dr. Phineas Quimby said in 1849: "Man is belief expressed."

While he was maintaining this attitude of mind, his attorney advised him that the opposing counsel had advised his clients not to pursue litigation further, as he felt they had no real evidence which would stand up in court. This was an answer to his prayer.

CHANGE YOUR THOUGHTS AND KEEP THEM CHANGED

Remember, there is no one to change but yourself. Change your attitude, your viewpoint; cease trying to change the world. The above-mentioned man realized it was his thought about the lawsuit and the relatives involved that really angered him—not other people and their actions. He suffered from his own judgment and reactions to their lies. When he ceased giving them power, he was able to give his allegiance to the Divine Presence within, Which knows all and sees all.

It is essential that you begin to awaken to the fact that you must cease blaming others for your confusion, sickness, or suffering; furthermore, discard that weird, superstitious belief that others are blocking your success. Your faith in God and all things good is your fortune, and success in your undertakings is assured.

CEASE BLAMING FATHER AND MOTHER

While talking with a man from Pakistan, who is a graduate from one of our universities here, he claimed that the reason he did not get ahead and was not promoted to higher echelons in the scientific field was that his father had constantly told him that he was a failure, was stupid, was a blockhead, and would never amount to anything.

It was true that his father had browbeaten him and had said all those things; but he began to understand the milieu in which he was reared and the customs of the times, plus the fact that his father didn't know any better and obviously didn't say all those things intentionally. Looking back, I pointed out that perhaps his father thought in his own way that his rebukes would stimulate and arouse him to go forth and be a better student.

I explained to him that he was now mature physically and emotionally but that it was essential that he become spiritually mature and realize that he was now responsible for the way he used his mind. It had nothing to do with his parents.

He began to realize that he was misusing and misdirecting his mental powers and that he alone was responsible for his habitual thinking and imagery. Accordingly, he began to fill his mind with the eternal verities, knowing that as he saturated his subconscious mind with the great truths of God, he would eradicate the negative patterns.

At my suggestion, he reiterated regularly several times a day: "Infinite Intelligence is guiding me. Divine law and order govern my life. Divine love fills my soul and I radiate love, peace, and goodwill to my parents and to all those around me. I forgive myself for harboring destructive, resentful thoughts, and I supplant them immediately with thoughts of harmony, peace, right action, and goodwill. I am God's son, and God is my boss, my guide, my counsellor, and my paymaster. Wonders are happening in my life."

This technique of prayer and a new attitude are now transforming his whole life. Spiritual maturity consists of knowing the laws of mind and applying the Creative Power constructively. It makes no difference what has happened in the past. You can change it now and become responsible for your own thoughts and actions.

He discovered that he, and he alone, was holding himself back—not his father, uncles, aunts, grandparents, or any others. It was negligence and apathy on his part. The Creative Principle was within him but he had failed to use It the right way. The Mind-Principle is timeless and spaceless. It makes no difference what has happened in the past. You can change it *now!*

Loose Them and Let Them Go

A woman who is an Executive Secretary is very disturbed because she felt humiliated by another woman in the office who introduced her to a visitor as a "File Clerk." I explained to her that the other woman had no power to demote her or to promote her and what she said or did had no power to disturb her in any way whatsoever. The disturbance was caused by the movement of her own mind; in other words, her thoughts about it.

If spiritually mature, you say to yourself: "Am I a File Clerk? Who am I?" You are an adult and you could say smilingly, "I was a File Clerk, but now I am promoted and am now an Executive Secretary." Spiritually, you can say to yourself, "I am a daughter of the Infinite and a child of Eternity. That is who I really am."

She learned to regard people objectively and not emotionally; she learned to let others be just as they are, and never to transfer the power in herself to another. This young woman learned to stand up for her rights, prerogatives, and privileges. She is now respected by everybody.

It is easy to correct a wrong introduction without rancor or bitterness; but it is wrong to be a doormat or a worm. If you think you are a worm, everybody is going to step on you. If the other woman is jealous of you, that is her problem, not yours. Loose her and let her go mentally and spiritually. Learn to laugh at yourself at least six times a day.

You Are the Master

And God said, Let us make man in our image, after our likeness: and let them have dominion over the fish of the sea, and over the fowl of the air, and over the cattle, and over all the earth, and over every creeping thing that creepeth upon the earth (Genesis 1:26).

This means that you are the master, not the slave. You have dominion and you must accept it and claim it. Cease transferring the power in yourself to external things. A man said to me after a lecture one Sunday at the Saddleback Theatre on El Toro Road in El Toro that he was terribly allergic to roses and that they affected his eyes, nose, and throat, bringing on inflammation of the mucosa, causing lachrymal effusions and distress.

I asked him if he had been born with this peculiar reaction to roses and he said, "No; it happened to me about five years previously." Apparently he had been engaged to a girl who

always wore red roses. She jilted him and he had subconsciously identified red roses with the girl, whom he still resented.

The rose is God's idea. God made it and pronounced his creation good. The rose is symbolic of beauty, order, symmetry, and proportion. It is made of the same substance as your blood stream. I explained to him that he must cease giving power to roses, pollen, timothy grass, or anything else. The rose has no power.

He learned to forgive his former girlfriend by releasing her to God and sincerely wishing for her all the blessings of life. Having done that, he is now able to meet his former girlfriend in his mind and no longer sizzles. He is now able to smell the rose, admire its beauty as God's creation, and now frequently wears one in his lapel.

He claimed his dominion. The cause was in his mind—not in the rose. The rose is harmless and never said to anyone: "If you handle me or smell me, I will give you hay fever." He ceased projecting qualities and properties onto the rose which the latter did not possess. The power is in you, not in the rose.

She Said, "Billy Does Not Want to Learn"

A mother was complaining to me that her son, Billy, eight years old, did not want to study and had no interest in school. In talking with Billy, it was discovered that the real trouble was that he did not like his teacher, because she said he was very slow and that he should wake up and try to learn something. Billy was resenting the teacher and fighting back in his own way.

The mother and father began to praise Billy, telling him

that they believed in him, that he had a wonderful mind, and that they knew he had it in him to shine in his studies and become outstanding some day. The mother interviewed the teacher, explaining to her diplomatically that if she let Billy know she believed in his ability and capacity to study and achieve, she was sure Billy would respond quickly, which he did.

It is well known that when parents or teachers believe in the ability and intelligence of a boy, he will advance much faster in his studies than he would if the parents or teachers did not show their faith in him to be, to do, and to have. Tell your daughters and sons that you believe in them; that God indwells them and that you see a magnificent future for each of them. Keep repeating these truths to them, knowing you are impregnating and conditioning their minds to greatness and victory. They will inevitably respond accordingly.

Your belief and conviction will be communicated to their impressionable minds and your expectancy will be fulfilled in Divine order. You are saluting the Divinity within them. Every time you do this, you are silently resurrecting the attributes and potentialities of the Infinite Being within them. They will fulfill your conviction of them because . . . *wisdom is justified of her children* (Matthew 11:19).

HE WAS HIS OWN PROBLEM

Recently I talked with a man who told me that he used to judge other people in the office regarding what they did and said and how they acted. This used to disturb and annoy him.

He used to be exercised and agitated about the way they lived. After he began to study Divine Science, however, he realized that he was projecting his own thoughts, opinions, and religious viewpoints onto them, and that the trouble was within himself. He was the cause of his own stomach trouble, the reason being that he found it difficult to tolerate their way of living, which contradicted his own conditioning and beliefs.

He said that the light of knowledge came to him and that instead of resenting their mode of living and their political and religious beliefs, he released them all to the Infinite and permitted them to believe whatever they wanted. He let them have their peculiarities, abnormalities, and unconventional ways. He realized there was no one to change but himself. Furthermore, he realized he was the cause of his own stomach distress, and consequently he no longer had to take barbiturates and sodium bicarbonate for relief. His changed attitude changed everything in his life.

He Said, "Oh, Some Day I Will Be Well"

The Bible says: . . . *Let the weak say, I am strong* (Joel 3:10). This man was claiming that he was weak, nervous, in poor health, and yet he wanted to be free from these ailments. Furthermore, he was stating that he will be free from these pains and aches sometime in the future. Such thoughts were blocking his good and preventing a healing.

The explanation is ofttimes the cure. I elaborated on the fact that when you say, "I AM," you are announcing first person, present tense. There is no future; therefore, you don't say,

"Some day I will be healed." The Infinite Healing Presence is within you. It has nothing to do with time or space. Give thanks for the healing taking place now. Your own consciousness is the door to all expression; therefore, you must claim that you are now what you long to be, and you will gradually establish the mental equivalent.

The will of the Infinite was expressed in the Bible in this way: . . . *And she answered, It is well* (II Kings 4:26); not "I will be well." When you say, "I shall be well some day" you are actually saying, "I am ill." Whatever you attach to "I AM" you become. Be careful, therefore, what you affix to "I AM."

At my suggestion, this man began to sing to himself, "I am all health; God is my health," knowing what he was doing and why he was doing it. Results followed. In about two weeks he was renewed, revitalized, and rejuvenated by the Holy Spirit within him.

You must realize that God's will is the recognition of that which is and not of that which will be. Peace is, joy is, love is, harmony is, wholeness is, right action is, wisdom is. God is the Eternal Now! timeless and spaceless. Claim your good now. Feel the reality of it and affirm boldly: "Thy will is done now."

The will of the Infinite is the nature of the Infinite and all the qualities, attributes, and potencies of God are within you now. When your wish or desire for harmony, health, peace, joy, or abundance becomes a conviction in your subconscious, then it is God's will and is no longer man's wish or choice. You know very well that your choice, intention, or desire must be felt as true, i.e., subjectified or impressed in your subconscious mind. When that happens, your will, which means your wish or choice, has become impressed in your deeper mind and will, therefore, be expressed.

In biblical language, it is no longer "my will" but "Thy will be done." Your conviction comes to pass (God's will). Your prayer is answered. This is a very simple explanation of . . . *Not my will, but thine, be done* (Luke 22:42).

SHE WAS AFRAID OF DOGS

A young woman told me that before she would ever accept an invitation to a home, she would first try to find out if they had a dog, as she feared and hated dogs. In talking with her, it was easy to see what had triggered this emotional response toward dogs. When she was about four years old a dog which she had been playing with bit her. The subconscious memory of that traumatic experience was the cause of her fear.

Love casts out fear, and at my suggestion she practiced the art of using her imagination in a constructive way. She would take a certain period every day, close her eyes, imagine a lively dog in front of her and proceed with her imaginary hands to fondly stroke the dog and rejoice mentally in the dog's reaction. She pictured herself giving the dog food and milk. She felt the naturalness and tangibility of all this, making it real and vivid.

In about a week's time she found herself free from this fear. She practiced the law of mind and discovered that what she dramatized subjectively entered into her subconscious mind and she found herself compelled to love dogs. Love casts out fear and love is an emotional attachment of your ideal, wherein you become fascinated, absorbed, and intensely interested in achieving a certain goal or objective in life.

In her imaginary act she also reflected on a dog's love for his master and how ofttimes he even gives his life for his master. She reflected and pondered on the faithfulness of dogs, such as how they rescue children and men lost in Alpine avalanches. All this would be looked upon as constructive meditation, building into her mentality a love for dogs.

In Quietness and in Confidence Shall Be Your Strength (Isaiah 30:15)

Today and almost every day we are reading reports and prognostications of Armageddon, the end of the world, starvation, revolution, and suggestions on how to fight cancer, tuberculosis, and pollution. Little or almost nothing is said about the pollution in the mind. "As within, so without."

We must cleanse the inside first. Moreover, what we fight against in our mind we magnify and we actually reinfect ourselves with more and more negativity. Man can continue to fight and destroy the slums, but he has forgotten that he must first cleanse the slums in the mind of man, for that is where the infection is. When the scientist gets still and quiet and contemplates an antidote, the answer comes to him in the relaxed, passive, receptive state of mind. He gets no answer by getting all excited and agitated about some problem, because he knows that such an attitude defeats itself and even makes matters worse.

THE QUIET MIND GETS THINGS DONE

Men and women who are seething within, full of anger at the establishment and other organizations, are not going to solve the problems of the world or cure anything regardless of all their activism, sloganeering, and outbursts of rage and hostility. Their emotions are self-destructive and lead to failure and disappointment.

If a president is to lead and accomplish things, it is necessary that he become still and contemplate the wisdom and power of God to lead and guide him. If you are the president of a company or are presiding at a PTA meeting, if you are quiet inside and in communion with the Infinite Presence within, you will be able to impart the quality of confidence, quietude, and peace to all those around you. Remember, whatever you are agitated about or quarrelling with in your mind is impregnating your subconscious and you are absorbing its negativity.

Come to a decision in your mind. Think quietly about the solution, the way out. Understand it; learn and know that you will become precisely what you contemplate. I am sure you don't want to become the image and likeness of the thing you are fighting mentally.

One woman said that she was terribly afraid of cancer. I asked her if it was doing anything to her. She said, "No." Then I suggested that she loose the idea and let it go. Think of wholeness, beauty, and perfection. I gave her the prayer previously mentioned: "I am all health; God is my health."

She broke that vicious thought by supplanting it with the real truth about her true self, which is God.

Many times during the day, quiet your mind. Think of God and His love. Claim peace, harmony, freedom, joy, power, wholeness, and strength, and your world will magically melt in the image and likeness of your contemplation.

THE CLOSED MIND

You can't put anything into a full cup or glass. A parachute is no good unless it opens up. Your mind must be open and receptive to new ideas, the eternal truths of life. The inflexible mind thinks it has all the truth; that it has a closed theology, a special revelation, and that there is nothing more to learn. Such a person is in a sad state. You are in the Presence of Infinity, and you can appropriate more wisdom, light, and understanding every day.

You are in the midst of an inexhaustible reservoir of infinite riches. Never in Eternity could you exhaust all the glories and wisdom of the Infinite One.

THE OLD LEGEND SAYS IT WELL

Millions of years ago the gods gathered together for a spiritual conclave on Mount Olympus. The purpose of the conference was to come to a decision as to whether ordinary mortals should be entrusted with the Truth so that they might be encouraged and stimulated to pattern their lives after the gods. The august decision was arrived at, and they decreed the "Jewel of Truth" be given to man.

One of the younger gods pleaded with his elders to give him the opportunity to go to earth so that he might convey the Precious Jewel to mankind and thereby win the blessings of the elder gods. Permission was granted him, and he was overwhelmed with joy to have this unparalleled opportunity. However, just as he was about to touch the earth, he stumbled and fell, and the "Jewel of Truth" was dashed to the ground and scattered into thousands of particles.

The gods on Mount Olympus were disturbed on hearing this and the younger god was abashed and disappointed. You can see the purpose of the legend, which points out that his fall caused lots of trouble. Forever after, men found particles of the jewel and each man fancied that he alone had found the Truth.

God is the Truth, and God indwells all men throughout the world. There is only One Truth, One Law, One Life, One Substance, and One Father of All—"Our Father"—the Life-Principle—Which is our common progenitor. Truth is one and indivisible. When you say "I AM," you are announcing the Presence and Power of God within you. This is the Reality of every person.

. . . *God is no respecter of persons* (Acts 10:34). When you name It, you cannot find It; and when you find It, you cannot name It.

14

Haunted House and Haunted Mind

THE HAUNTED HOUSE WAS IN HIS MIND

Recently I had an interesting conversation with a man who claimed that his country home was haunted. He rarely goes there now. The shutters are drawn and the windows are barred. He said that the beautiful Persian rugs are being eaten up by moths and other insects. He says that he does not believe in ghosts, and even though he jests about it, he is actually afraid to sleep there at night.

This goes to show that everybody believes in something, whether it be a religion or a false god. Many atheists say, "I do not believe in God"; but they acknowledge some other ruler of their mind. Every dominant thought in your mind which you accept and believe to be true is a ruler over you.

In England and in many parts of our own country, you read from time to time of houses being haunted, of peculiar noises, ghosts walking around, lights going on and off, furniture being moved, windows opened, icy gusts of wind, and other eerie happenings.

This man had bought the country home some years ago and in the beginning had spent many happy weekends there. After some months, though, the neighbors told him about a rumor that a great tragedy had taken place in his home. The former owners who had sold the home to him had never mentioned this fact to him. Others enlarged upon the story, and each one's guess or report was as good as the other.

Following these reports, strange occurrences suddenly began to take place in his home, causing him to believe it was haunted by evil entities and earthbound spirits. There were words spoken to him, and he didn't really know what they meant. Ghosts move around when the light in the mind is not clear. The ghosts he experienced were creatures of his fears and ignorance, which is darkness of the mind.

The Cure

Many times the explanation is the cure. I pointed out to him that he was actually a victim of negative suggestions because for two months he had no problems, and then the minute he accepted the negative suggestions of his neighbors his subconscious dramatized his fears and superstitions. All things that hurt or harm love the darkness and hate the light. The cure was to raise the shades in his mind and let in the sunshine of Divine love.

All the things of darkness walk at night. Many people report seeing ghosts and spectres, or imagine they do, when passing a graveyard at night. They have illusions of the mind due to fear and false beliefs. This happens frequently at twilight when the light is fading and the shadows fall.

One man walking near his home at night imagined he saw a man mounted on a black horse who was aiming a rifle at him. He stood still, paralyzed by fear, completely immobilized. When his wife, who was expecting his arrival, opened the door of the home, the light from his home revealed a peculiar branching of the trees, which had appeared to his mind as the shape of a man on a horse with a gun. This is what the twilight did to this man, to cite one example.

He wondered why the tables began to move now, why the lights go on and off, when he visits his country home. All this was the working of his own subconscious mind. His mind was a haunted house based on his acceptance of the negative suggestions.

I gave him the following spiritual prescription, which he was to repeat out loud several times a day, particularly at night: "My home is known in Divine Mind. God's peace fills and saturates the atmosphere of my home. Divine love comes in the door and Divine love goes out the door. My life is God's life, and God's peace fills my mind and heart. My faith is in God, and all things good. God cares for me. I am immersed in the sacred circle of God's love. Divine love surrounds me and enfolds me, and I bear a charmed life. The light of God shines in me, and God's love saturates the atmosphere of my home. Divine law and order prevail."

This prayer neutralized the negative suggestions given him by the neighbors, and he soon learned that the ghosts he had feared were created in the gloomy galleries of his own mind.

THE PAST IS DEAD

I have discovered through talking with many people that while they have moved their bodies to another city or state, they have never moved their minds, which makes a vast difference. They failed to realize that they could not run away from their minds. They experienced loss of love, a death had taken place, or some scandal had occurred in the household. Living in the past is deadly, as it blights their hopes and aspirations and robs them of vitality and peace of mind.

Many fail to see that they are preserving these traumatic shocks or memories in their subconscious mind. I have discovered that many go back and relive them every night, and they suffer from nightmares and unpleasant dreams. There are skeletons in the closet of the mind that many return to every night. They have to learn to walk away from the past without any sense of attachment whatsoever. They must learn to change their thoughts and to keep them changed.

What do you think about yourself? What do you think about the world? the news? Do conditions make you angry? If so, you have installed a bad ruler over your mind. It makes no difference if all the men who write in the newspapers or who present news over the various media are wrong and you alone are right. If what they say irritates you and makes you upset, you have installed a bad ruler over your household.

You are always living in your state of mind. You are not living where your body is. Actually, you are living in the state of consciousness, which is the sum total of all your thoughts, feelings, and beliefs.

There was a woman here in Laguna Hills mourning the loss of her mother. Every day she would go to the grave and place flowers on it and cry. Her mother wasn't there, though. She was not in that body in the ground, which was gradually undergoing dissolution and returning to its primordial elements. All this sadness, gloom, and melancholia was in the daughter's mind, and she felt a sense of loss and was gradually losing her vision. She got a morbid pseudo-satisfaction out of all this. She was identifying with cessation, limitation, and finality, all of which infected her mind. She was experiencing loss of health, wealth, love, and practically everything else was going wrong because she was in the mood of loss.

She learned to change her attitude after a time and realized her mother was with her, separated by frequency only. She began to pray for her mother by rejoicing in her mother's new birthday in God and radiating love, peace, joy, and goodwill to her. Every time her mother came into her mind, she would affirm: "Mother, your journey is onward, upward, and Godward." Gradually the eyesight came back and her whole life was transformed by scientific prayer. Prayer changes the person who prays.

HE HAD A MARTYR COMPLEX

While holding a conference with a man in my study, he said that he was shabbily treated by the corporation for which he had worked over twenty-five years. He seemed to love to recite and indulge in the mental ruminations of how unjust and unfair they had been to him and how, when the company merged with another, they let him go with no explanation. He was building up a sort of a martyr complex, and his morbidity and resentment had expressed itself in an acute case of high blood pressure.

I explained to him that he had placed a gangster in charge of his mind, a tyrannical ruler which was playing havoc with his health and finances.

TAKING A JOURNEY IN THE MIND

I explained to him that he was always travelling in his mind and that whatever dominant idea governs the mind sinks into the subconscious and returns as experience and events.

The following is the technique he decided to use: "I loose the organization completely and surrender them to God and wish them well. Infinite Spirit opens up a new door of expression for me in a wonderful way. I am now giving of my talents and experience in a magnificent way, and I know what I accept and believe in my mind will come to pass. I am going on a mental journey from desire to fulfillment. This new idea I now possess grows internally and comes forth as manifestation."

This dominant idea which now governed him also governed all his lesser thoughts, ideas, and emotions. It became his ruler and governor. As he continued to affirm these truths, he succeeded in saturating his subconscious and a new door for an overseas appointment suddenly came into his experience with a far greater income than he had ever experienced.

RELIGION AND SCIENCE

Your religion should be accompanied by science. Religion and science are two arcs of a circle which unite and complete the circle. Religion must be scientific, and science must be religious, or there is no real meeting ground. Man's mind becomes a sort of haunted house when he dwells on old regrets, tragedies, traumatic events, and other unfortunate experiences.

When man learns that there are laws of the mind which induce a response from the Infinite Spirit when rightly operated, and when he is convinced of that, he shall experience the joy of the answered prayer.

HE HEARD EERIE SCREECHING VOICES

A man who had hated his wife for years, felt a great sense of guilt, after she died of cancer, for the shabby way he had treated her. He feared he would be punished and he had a deep sense of remorse. He told me that at night he would hear weird noises, eerie screeching of unearthly voices and footsteps on the stairs. He saw what he believed to be ghosts walking in his bedroom. He would hear the creaking of the floor boards and clanking of chains. He claimed that invisible hands clawed him at night, and he had scratches to prove it. These experiences took place between 12:00 and 3:00 every night. The doctor had given him tranquilizers, but they did not help him.

I had several sessions with this man, and it was clear to me that he had been dabbling with the Ouija Board, attending séances, and he believed in all sorts of evil entities. He felt a deep sense of remorse and was in the throes of deep depression, all caused by his sense of guilt.

I explained to him that there are no ghosts, goblins, spectres, or eerie screechings or abnormal noises in a house (mind) of meditation on the truths of God. These phenomena do not occur in the mind that is filled with the sunlight of God's truth and God's love. The deep sense of guilt plus his fear of punishment and belief in evil entities caused his subconscious to dramatize and bring forth all these experiences.

Understanding gives you strength and may be called the sun, which dissipates the fog and confusion in the mind. Raise the shades and the sunlight streams in. You have peace when you become aware of your spiritual strength. That is the peace that knows no enemies outside because it knows none within.

This man decided to release his wife and to give beauty for ashes. Night and day he affirmed that God's love filled her soul and that God's peace reigned supreme in her mind. After a week or so he was at peace about her and felt guilty no longer. Then he began to saturate his mind with the 91st and 23rd Psalms several times a day, particularly at night prior to sleep.

The healing power of God was released through him as he affirmed the great truths of the Psalms. Peace came to his mind and he heard no more noises. He surrendered himself and his wife to God. When the light and love of God entered his soul, all the darkness disappeared.

LET WISDOM GOVERN

Enthrone in your mind wisdom, which is an awareness of the Presence and Power of God, by dwelling on the concept of peace, strength, joy, and right action. Busy your mind with these truths and you will experience harmony and satisfaction in your mental house. You are here to manifest, portray, and dramatize the nature of God in human action here in the flesh. Job said, . . . *Yet in my flesh shall I see God* (Job 19:26).

SHE CLAIMED A NOISY GHOST WAS THE TROUBLE

Having had a long conversation with a woman from San Francisco, I deduced from the interview that her daughter was the so-called ghost. She experimented and sent her daughter to her grandmother in Los Angeles. In her two-week absence, there were no episodes of dishes being moved, tables overturned, and pictures falling off the walls, lights being turned off or windows opened.

Poltergeist activity is well-known all over the world and is a real phenomenon of the subconscious mind. It has nothing to do with ghosts or evil entities. The cause is well-known and is simply a psychokinetic force latent in the deeper mind, and ofttimes it becomes manifested at times of stress or puberty.

When talking with her daughter, age twelve, who had been brought to my study by her grandmother, I found she was terribly resentful of her mother and felt that her mother preferred her brother and had even told her so. She had asked her mother on the onset of her menstruation what it meant, and her mother had said that it was the dirty age for girls. She was getting even with her mother with the ghostly activity. The paranormal phenomena were manifestations of the power of her subconscious mind, which she used negatively.

There is only One Power, and we can use it constructively or negatively. I explained the situation to the mother and grandmother. The mother shows love and attention to her daughter now and assures her that she is wanted, loved, and appreciated. The little girl learned to pray for her mother by realizing frequently: "God loves my mother. I love her, and she loves me." She has made this into a sort of song and sings it silently and audibly many times a day.

The answer to all human relation problems is to exalt God in one another. You can't think of two things at the same time. The answer is to think of God and His love.

THE WEATHER GIVES HIM A COLD

A man said to me that the room was warm and when he went out into the night air he began to sneeze and felt chilly and began to cough. He blamed the weather. The cough and the chills from which he suffered seemed to confirm his belief that it was due to the night air that he caught a cold. He said that his temperature went up and he used nose drops and aspirin.

I explained to him that the night air did not give him a cold. The atmosphere is innocuous and has no power to give a cold to anyone. The cold was due to his belief and not to the air. When he moved from a rather hot room to the cool night air there was a change of temperature and nature sought a balance, resulting in his sneezing. This was nature's way of bringing about an adjustment. He made an effect a cause and brought on his own suffering as a result.

The cosmic laws are providential and are working for the good of all. This man misinterpreted the sneezing, which was merely a reflex induced by the subconscious mind to adjust the temperature of the body. For every action there is an equal and corresponding reaction proportionate to the action. This is physics and also metaphysics.

Many people, when they first begin to cough a little, become fearful that they are catching a cold, and what they fear they attract. Emotional excitement is the action and a sneeze or a cough is the reaction. This completes the cycle and there is no further result. If, through ignorance or fear, we believe that the sneeze or cough is a signal that a severe cold is on the way, our belief brings on the illness we feared.

For the thing which I greatly feared is come upon me . . . (Job 3:25). Change it and affirm: "That which I greatly love comes upon me." Fall in love with harmony, health, peace, abundance, and the truths of God. The desert of your life will then rejoice and blossom as the rose.

15

Getting Acquainted with the Language of the Bible

The Two Sides

It is said that there are two sides to every question, but only one right side. You must learn what the right side is in order to know the Truth. Emerson said, in his essay on Compensation:" . . . for inevitable dualism bisects all nature, so that each thing is a half, and suggests another thing to make it whole; as, spirit, matter; man, woman; subjective, objective; in, out; upper, lower; motion, rest; yea, nay."

There are light and darkness, ebb and flow, in and out, sweet and sour. Darkness is absence of light. There is heat and there is cold, but from the standpoint of absolute Truth, there is no cold. All opposites are reconciled in the Absolute. There are health and sickness, but in the Absolute all is wholeness, beauty, and perfection. The positive value is light, health, and love. The opposites are portrayed in our experiences so that we may learn the significance of the positives. Without the opposite or negative to background the positive, we would not become aware of the latter in its true significance.

When people ask the question: Why did God create us? So that we could err? make mistakes? become ill? Why good and evil? pain and sickness? The above is the answer. We know things by contrast, by comparisons. How would we know what joy was unless we could shed from time to time a tear of sorrow?

We are sentient beings, and we recognize colors because of their different light vibrations. Infinite differentiation is the law of life. True scientific knowledge recognizes the opposites in life. The good has its opposite in order that we may choose the good and reject the negative. To choose and understand the good in life is called wisdom. Wisdom knows what is right and what conforms to universal truth.

We might say that there are two languages. The Bible is written in a secret language of parables, allegories, metaphors, and figurative language. The world speaks another language, and millions take the Bible literally. Laws of the country are written in English, but there is constant controversy among lawyers as to what they mean. The Supreme Court is divided as to the meaning of parts of the Constitution, yet it is written in English. The politicians in California say the tide is turning for them. They do not mean that literally, although I suppose some may take it that way.

There are two languages in the Bible, and this results in endless confusion and misinterpretation. You must learn the meaning of symbols in order to understand the Bible. Paul speaks of . . . *Christ in you, the hope of glory* (Colossians 1:27). Christ is not a man. The statement means the Presence of

God in every person. When you begin to use this Power, you come into a new understanding of yourself.

Christ is called the wisdom which Jesus found enabling him to do great things. This knowledge is the producer of health and happiness. When you know that thoughts are things and that whatever you think and feel to be true is expressed in your life, and when you know that whatever you imagine you become, you then possess a part of the wisdom called Christ.

The Christ in you simply means the practice of the Presence of God. It has nothing to do with personality. The God-Presence is no respecter of persons. The average man does not know about this Divine Presence within himself and believes that external things affect him and influence him without his consent. This attitude is called the son of perdition in the Bible, which means a sense of loss and limitation.

Knowledge is what a man knows, and what man in general knows is, unfortunately, not the Divinity within. God is a synonym for good, and the contemplation of all things good brings health and happiness.

Ask yourself if that which you fear is real or illusionary. When you claim right action, beauty, love, peace, and Divine inspiration and harmony, and when these truths, powers, and qualities of God are functioning in your life, that is called the Christ in you, the hope of glory.

Someone asked me the other day what Paul meant by . . . *The day of Christ* . . . (II Thessalonians 2:2). Paul is not talking about a millennium when all men will be suddenly and miraculously transformed by the Light from On High. Illumination does not come that way. It comes to individuals through meditation, prayer, and mystic visioning. No one can give it to you. It is not something that can be conveyed to you apart from your mental participation and attention to the eternal verities of life.

There must be, as Paul says, a falling away first, which means the falling away and eradication of all false beliefs and erroneous concepts before the Presence of God is felt in the heart. As long as you are convinced of powers outside yourself that condition your life, you are full of the world's beliefs and knowledge. If you want the knowledge and wisdom called Christ in the Bible, you must give up false religious beliefs and the propaganda of the world and accept the gift of Truth in your heart now.

Paul says: . . . *Except there come a falling away first.* . . (II Thessalonians 2:3). This means that when the popular theories and dogmatic beliefs of the world knowledge are revealed to your mind for what they are—thieves and robbers of your happiness—then the day of Christ, or awakening to the Truth, will come to you.

It is useless and foolish to say you believe in God and at the same time believe in a power to thwart the action of God. There must be no compromise, equivocation, or vacillation on this point. Externals are not causative. To believe that others may mar your happiness or to accept the fact that you have an incurable condition is to foster a belief that is a thief and a robber, depriving you of health and happiness.

THE AVERAGE BELIEF

It seems very reasonable for the ordinary man to believe that the things which cause sickness are outside and the things which heal are also outside. In this way he has developed the idea that he catches a "disease," not realizing that disease is an emotional disturbance which manifests itself on the flesh.

I have frequently referred to your subconscious mind, which faithfully records all your emotions. Your body is the plastic disc upon which the result is recorded. The body has no power in and of itself, but it faithfully reproduces whatever is impressed upon it. Anything you believe is indelibly written in your subconscious mind and appears in your body and affairs.

All this is a part of the wisdom called Christ. There is a science of the mind which distinguishes between Truth and error, and when you come to a definite conclusion in your mind that there is only One Power, wonders will happen in your life.

THE SERPENT

The serpent in the Bible represents the five senses and the judging according to appearances. The seed of the serpent is fear and false knowledge. The serpent comes quickly and noiselessly; and before you are aware of its presence in the jungle, it strikes quickly. The suggestions and false beliefs of the world mind leave a sting in the undisciplined mind and bring on all manner of trouble.

THE ANSWER TO ALL PROBLEMS

The answer to all the problems of the world is to follow the injunction of the Bible: *Trust in the Lord with all thine heart; and lean not unto thine own understanding. In all thy ways acknowledge him, and he shall direct thy paths* (Proverbs 3:5–6).

16

Many Answers to Your Many Questions

SPIRIT AND MATTER are one, and modern science today speaks only of the interconvertibility of energy and matter. Energy is a term used by science for Spirit, or God. Many people today deny the existence of God, or the Living Spirit Almighty. We also have groups here on the West Coast of the United States who even deny matter.

We are living in a subjective and an objective world. There are two ends of a stick. The formless takes form, the invisible becomes visible. The ancients said that God becomes man by believing Himself to be man. All of us are manifestations of the Infinite Spirit. We are here to discover our Divinity.

Paul says, . . . *Therefore, glorify God in your body* . . . (I Corinthians 6:20). Spirit needs form to express Itself. Your body is a vehicle enabling you to express the wonders and glories within you.

SHOULD I GO TO AN ASHRAM?

A sincere young girl from a local college who is deeply spiritual asked me if I thought it advisable for her to go to India and enter an Ashram in order to get away from the rat race, as there was so much conflict in college, drug abuses, sexual aberrations of all kinds, and some of her teachers of philosophy had claimed there was no God.

I explained to her that I had been to many Ashrams in India and had spoken there but that it is not necessary to go to India to find God, for God indwells her, and walks and talks in her. She could practice the Presence of God on Broadway, New York City, or on Hollywood Boulevard in Los Angeles, as well as in her own home, in the college, or in the street or marketplace.

I explained to her that true wisdom and spiritual growth do not consist in running away from where she is to some foreign shore. On the contrary, her task and duty is to live where she is, complete her studies, and learn to contribute of her talents to the world. The "world" in which she was living is the mass mind, and she must learn to *come out from among them, and be ye separate* (II Corinthians 6:17).

She learned to pray scientifically by disciplining her thoughts and by radiating love and goodwill to all the students and teachers. I gave her a book of meditations entitled *Quiet Moments with God** and suggested that she saturate her mind night and morning with one of the sixty meditations in

---

* *Quiet Moments with God* by Dr. Joseph Murphy, DeVorss and Company, Inc., Marina del Rey, California, 1956.

the book, knowing that as she reconditioned her mind, her whole perspective of life would change, and it did. She began to think, speak, and act from the Divine Center within herself, not from the superimposed structure of fear, ignorance, and superstition.

FOOLISH BELIEFS

Many people have weird, grotesque beliefs about money, possessions, and earthly amusements. You are here to have recreation, love in your life, and the full expression of your talents. There is no reason why you should not have a wonderful home, the best possible clothes, a wonderful car, and literally the best of everything. . . . *God, who giveth us richly all things to enjoy* (I Timothy 6:17).

You are not possessed by external riches; neither do you give undue importance to them. God possesses all, but you have the use of all the comforts of life while on this plane. You know that God is the Source of all things, and you look to the Source for all your blessings because you know your security and happiness is not in external accumulations or possessions but in your conviction of God's goodness and God's riches in the land of the living.

Never separate Spirit from matter. You are living in both worlds, and you are here to lead a balanced and harmonious life. We find some non-thinking people condemning material things, money, land, automobiles, gold, and diamonds. Many, however, will not wear gold, considering it to be a sin. Of course, there are crime, misery, suffering, and injustice in the world; but these are due to man's destructive and negative thinking.

God made the world and all things in the cosmos and pronounced everything good. It is frightfully stupid to call God, the "All Good," and the world ugly. This creates a conflict in the mind, resulting in confusion and mental disturbance. The world is Spirit made manifest in multitudinous forms.

A man asked me the other day what Gandhi meant when he said, "Renounce the world and take it back in different terms." When he spoke of the world, he did not mean sticks, stones, trees, lakes, etc. What he referred to in this statement was the mass mind, the dull, opinionated, confused, irrational thinking of four billion people in this world.

You renounce and completely reject the false beliefs, fears, ignorance, and superstitions of the mass mind, the great psychic sea, in which all of us are immersed. You renounce it when you begin to think right, feel right, do right, and act right and pray right. By prayer, we mean the contemplation of the truths of God from the highest standpoint.

You become what you contemplate, and by dwelling on the attributes, qualities, and potencies of the Infinite within you, you are no longer in the world, or mass mind. You are then in tune with the Infinite, and you are living at higher levels of consciousness, enabling you to find peace in this changing world.

REBELLION AGAINST TAXES

I received a letter recently asking me to send a donation to a certain group who said it is unlawful to pay taxes. The writer of the letter quoted the Constitution to back up his argument. All this, of course, is so much folderol. You know that this question was asked two thousand years ago. . . . *Is it lawful to give tribute unto Caesar . . . ?* (Matthew 22:17). Jesus knew what the motive of the question was, because he could read the mind of the interrogator.

The people in that era were under the Roman domination. They chafed, resented, and hated the tax collectors of that day; however, they were compelled to pay taxes to Caesar, or Rome. If Jesus had answered in the negative, he would have been advocating rebellion against the Roman government, and, consequently, would be subject to arrest and imprisonment. He said: . . . *Render therefore unto Caesar the things which are Caesar's; and unto God the things that are God's* (Matthew 22:21).

Caesar represents the world in which we live. We have to pay tribute to Caesar and fulfill the demands of Caesar. We are here to express ourselves, clothe ourselves, feed ourselves, wash ourselves, and contribute our talents to the world. All of us are interdependent. The carpenter, the plumber, the doctor, the pharmacist, the lawyer, the farmer, the teacher, and the engineer are all needed. Furthermore, we have to contribute taxes to support the local, state, and federal governments.

The government has no money except that which it extracts from the people. Officials may not use it wisely, but nevertheless, in an ordered society, all of us have to contribute to Caesar. The world demands of you your skill, your talents, your abilities, and your labor. Your family demands protection, loving care, and all the necessities of life. You must pay tribute to Caesar and put your shoulder to the wheel. Make this world a better place in which to live for yourself and your posterity.

The most important thing in the world is to put God first in your life. God is the Supreme Cause, the Creator of the world, and He is the Progenitor of all mankind and the entire cosmos. Every morning and evening, set aside some time for a visit with God—your Higher Self.

Commune with this Presence and know that your thought and feeling control your destiny. Claim Divine law and order in your life and realize that Divine love and Divine peace are moving through all your actions and all the experiences of your life. Affirm boldly: "Divine law and harmony govern my mind, my body, and all my undertakings. Wonders are happening in my life."

HANDLING THAT BURDEN

When you feel frustration and obstructions to your good in life are apparent, then render to God the things that are God's, which means to pray according to universal principles. Pray this way: Think about the Infinite Intelligence, Boundless Wisdom, Absolute Harmony, and Supreme Power within you; then claim, "Divine freedom is mine, Divine peace is mine, and there is a Divine harmonious solution taking place now." Be constantly aware that Infinite Spirit knows the way and reveals the solution, and you will soon find the answer in your physical world.

When you tune in with the Infinite, your spiritual thoughts will transform your physical or material world and redeem it from sorrow, lack, and limitation, bringing beauty and order into your world.

Do You Serve Communion?

Since the first Sunday in November, 1976, I have been speaking at the Saddleback Cinema Theatre, 23682 El Toro Road, El Toro, California. A woman called me on the phone recently and asked if we serve Holy Communion. Many people mean by Holy Communion consecrated wafers and wine, all of which are purely symbolic and which represent your thought and feeling, the idea and the emotion, the Spirit and form.

Bread represents the bread of life, such as the thought of peace, joy, love, goodwill, courage, faith, and confidence. Without that you cannot live nobly in this confused world. Wine represents the exhilaration of the Holy Spirit in you, i.e., the Spirit of goodness, truth, and beauty moving on the waters of your mind and the emanation of goodwill to all.

Bread is the Divine idea in your mind, and the wine means that you animate, vitalize, and emotionalize the idea so that it is impressed in your subconscious mind and becomes manifest in your life. The thought and the thing are one. Spirit needs a body in which to express Itself. Divine life and Divine substance are one. You can't separate Spirit from form. The whole world is God made manifest in countless forms. Everything you see came out of the mind of man or the mind of God, which is really the same thing, for there is only one mind.

We must not despise or criticize material things. You are composed of Spirit and matter yourself, and you must demonstrate what you believe in. You must, therefore, show forth your results by your daily communion with the Divine Presence within you. As you meditate on the qualities, attributes, and potencies of the Infinite, you will feel the Spirit of God moving on your behalf, animating, sustaining, and strengthening you.

When you experience this Divine transfusion taking place within you, then you can rest assured you are partaking of Holy Communion, because you are communing with wholeness, beauty, love, and peace in the silence of your own soul. You must demonstrate what you believe. Remember, though, you are what you contemplate. Contemplate whatsoever things are true, lovely, noble, and God-like. This is Holy Communion.

THE DIGNITY OF LABOR

During a speaking engagement at the Unity Church in New Orleans, operated by Dr. Ruth Murphy and her lovely daughter, I had a consultation with a prominent business woman, who told me that she has great difficulty hiring men to mow the lawn, clean the horse stables, etc. Furthermore, the maids she has for her large household refuse to do certain types of work in the house, believing it to be degrading and demeaning. One maid, for example, refused to do the laundry, so she had to get a Chinese man who came and was glad to do the work with a song in his heart. She said he took a delight in his work and brought forth spotless clothes for her inspection.

No work is degrading. We are here to do all things for the glory of God, whether it be washing windows, cleaning the floor, or cleaning out the stable. There is no such thing as menial labor, as it is the Spirit, or God, operating in and through the bodies of all men and women throughout the world. A dead man cannot wash the floor or clean the bathroom: The Life Principle has left him. It is God working in you and through you, no matter what you do.

You can misdirect the Divine Energy in you, or you can use it constructively. No matter what your assignment is in life, realize that it is God in action. By that you mean God is thinking, speaking, and acting through you, and wonders will happen in your life as a result.

RELIGION IS THE PRACTICE OF THE PRESENCE

Recently I counseled a man who had a suppurating wound in his leg, which emitted a very foul odor. I sent him to a local physician who has the reputation of praying regularly for his patients.

I explained to this man that God is the Holy Spirit within him and that It could cleanse, heal, and restore his leg to wholeness and beauty. He prayed for his doctor also, realizing he was Divinely guided to do the right thing. His simple prayer was: "The Holy Spirit remolds and reshapes all the tissues of my leg to beauty, order, and symmetry so that in my flesh I shall see God's wholeness made manifest."

The doctor dressed his wound and told him to continue claiming, "God is healing me now." The doctor did not look down his nose at the man, but he realized that the Infinite Healing Presence could rearrange the atoms of his body to wholeness and perfection. In a short time, this man had a remarkable healing. This doctor did not think that he was degrading himself by cleaning out the stable in the mind of this man or in removing the pus from the wound.

The Bible says: . . . *If I wash thee not, thou hast no part with me* (John 13:8). This refers to Jesus washing the feet of his disciples. Feet means understanding, and the disciples are your faculties of mind. It is incumbent, therefore, on everyone to open the mind and heart and let in the cleansing healing power of the Holy Spirit.

Wherever disease, lack, and misery are present, no matter how loathsome the sickness may be, the Holy Spirit can restore, heal, and reintegrate the atoms of the body into God's pattern of wholeness and vitality. This is the practice of the Presence of God, which is true religion. When you give yourself a transfusion of God's grace and love, you are truly partaking of holy communion in the same way that a piece of bread you eat is transmuted into tissue, muscle, bone, and blood in your body.

THE HARLOTS OF THE BIBLE

We are all harlots when we cohabit with evil, such as resentment, hate, jealousy, and hostility, in our mind. These negative emotions spawn an evil progeny, bringing about all manner of disease and mental conflict.

In a recent lecture at the Saddleback Valley Plaza Cinema, Laguna Hills, I pointed out that I had conducted many marriages for women who had walked the primrose path. They had eventually completely transformed their lives, however, and had married wonderful men, and were presently leading upright and wonderful lives. Some of these women asked me if they might meet former customers who might inform their husbands of their past.

I explained that inasmuch as they had forgiven themselves and were leading God-like lives now and had ceased accusing themselves, no man could accuse them or trouble them. . . . *Where are those thine accusers? hath no man condemned thee? She said, No man, Lord. And Jesus said unto her, Neither do I condemn thee: go, and sin no more* (John 8:10–11).

They understood the meaning of this part of the Scripture and realized that the past is dead and that nothing matters but this moment. A new beginning is a new end.

The Bible says that Jesus consorted with harlots and publicans. *The Son of man is come eating and drinking; and ye say, Behold a gluttonous man, and a wine-bibber, a friend of publicans and sinners!* (Luke 7:34). The reason is obvious. The harlot has sunk to the depths of degradation. She is despised and ostracized by society. But ofttimes these same people are most receptive to the Truth. They are hungry and thirsty for the eternal truths of life. They rejoice at hearing that God never condemns and that all they have to do is to change

their thoughts and keep them changed and then their subconscious will respond. The past is forgotten and remembered
no more.

Perfunctory prayer will not suffice; but a real inner transformation of the mind and heart where the woman has an
intense desire to become a daughter of the Infinite and a true
child of eternity, when that inner change takes place in her,
the law of her subconscious being compulsive, she is compelled to lead a new life dramatizing loyalty, love, honesty,
and integrity. . . . *Their sins and their iniquities will I remember
no more* (Hebrews 8:12).

THE PHARISEES OF THE WORLD

The Pharisee is everywhere. He is the type of person who
follows rituals, ceremonies, liturgies, and the tenets of his
church. He takes a wafer and some wine and thinks he is
communing with God. The bread is still a piece of flour and
the wine is the distilled essence of grapes, and he thinks to
partake of these is holy communion. He may follow all the
rules and regulations of his church and feel he belongs to the
right religion.

He is usually proud and beautiful on the outside and may
be conventionally good, but the only important thing is the
belief in his heart. The lip service to some prescribed doctrine, dogma, or creed is meaningless. The eternal verities
must be felt sincerely as true in our hearts. The prayers used
must be full of Spirit and Life and not mere mechanical rec-
itations without understanding or love in the heart.

Woe unto you, scribes and Pharisees, hypocrites! for ye are like unto whited sepulchres, which indeed appear beautiful outward, but are within full of dead men's bones, and of all uncleanness (Matthew 23:27).

Nothing Good or Bad

Shakespeare said: "There is nothing good or bad, but thinking makes it so." The only real good or bad is in our own thought about the thing, the process, the condition, the plant, or the flower. Many people touch poison ivy and poison oak and they have no reaction whatsoever. They have a good relationship with all plants. Others have the thought that poison ivy is dangerous and poisonous, and even though they may be four or five feet away from it and don't even touch it, they get the reaction of their thought.

Their subconscious knows that they fear it, and what they fear they experience. *For the thing which I greatly feared is come upon me* . . . (Job 3:25).

Her Mother Said She Was a Sinner

A few weeks ago I conducted a seminar at Unity Church, Phoenix, which is operated by Reverend Blaine Mays, one of the most outstanding ministers of New Thought in this country.

A woman visited me at the hotel complaining that her mother was condemning her because she played cards, danced, went to the movies, took a cocktail now and then, and ate meat. The explanation ofttimes is the cure. Her mother was speaking from the stand point of ignorance, fear and superstition. Her mother was brainwashed by some cult and was projecting her taboos and prohibitions onto her daughter. This young woman was thirty years old, had not married and was afraid of sex, of men, and was full of conflicts.

I suggested that she go out and do all the things she had been told not to do. As Emerson said: "Do the things you are afraid to do, and the death of fear is certain." I suggested to her that she explain to her mother in definite, concrete terms that she would no longer take any instructions from her and that she was a choosing, volitional being and would come to decisions in her own life about her clothes, her food, her companionship, and all other phases of her life.

There is a Guiding Principle within her which responds to her thought. The evil was in the mind of her mother, for there is no evil in cards, in wine or dancing, or having a date with a young man. She came to a decision and cleansed her mind of all these foolish, stupid proscriptions of her mother and decided to lead her own life, taking God as her partner, guide, and counsellor.

Since then I have received a letter from her saying that the sense of freedom was wonderful, and that she is now engaged to a young dentist. In her words, they are madly in love and she is looking out through the eyes of love. All nature has taken on a new hue. She is dedicating her thoughts, desires, and actions to Truth, realizing that Divine law and order govern her life.

As she continues to practice the law of harmony and love,

she will go forward to victory, fulfillment, and achievement. . . .
And the desert shall rejoice, and blossom as the rose (Isaiah 35:1).

A Visit from Las Vegas

An old friend of mine visited me from Las Vegas. She proceeded to tell of all the tests she had had made by her allergist. She said that she was sensitive to dog hair, cat hair, eggs, dust, pollen, and trees of all kinds.

I pointed out to her how a doctor friend of mine had healed a woman who was allergic to red roses. He got some synthetic roses from one of the Woolworth stores and placed them on his waiting room table prior to her entry. She had an acute attack and was angry that he had the roses on the table. He explained to her that they were synthetic, and she laughed. Both of them had a good laugh, and suddenly she realized that the whole problem was in her mind. She had no further trouble with red or white roses after that.

Many people are allergic to their wives, husbands, or the fellow next to them on the bench. If you hypnotize a man who says he is allergic to timothy grass or ragweed or pollen and put a glass of distilled water under his nose, telling him this is timothy grass, he will get all the symptoms, indicating that the allergic belief is hidden in the recesses of his subconscious mind.

I explained to my friend from Las Vegas about my recent trip to India, Nepal, and other places. In banks in the street, you will see people there suffering from various ailments, their hands oozing from suppurating wounds. They give change in rupees to fellow natives and also to tourists. These rupees handled by the various vendors in the stores and banks were absolutely filthy and undoubtedly laden with all manner of virulent germs, yet nobody had any reaction. It is obvious that no one is allergic to money. They seem to have made peace with all kinds of money—tainted or otherwise.

A medical doctor in India told me that during the bubonic plague, when many died like flies, people stole money from the dead and no one seemed to get the disease. Apparently their spiritual attunement with money neutralized all toxic bacilli and virulent organisms.

Acquaint now thyself with him, and be at peace . . . (Job 22:21).

17

Things You Should Know

RECENTLY A WOMAN asked me if it was a sign of insanity to talk to oneself. Apparently, her husband engages in this act occasionally. I explained to her that talking to oneself is not unusual and is not necessarily a sign of insanity. Her husband was merely reacting to the pressures of his business.

Basically, the reaction is caused by the sensing of the two selves in each of us; namely, the spiritual and the human, or five-sense man. Children often chatter with invisible playmates, which is explained by some psychologists as a keener sense of the subjective self. In many circles the psychic explanation of the reaction is put forth and accepted.

WHY HE TALKED TO HIMSELF

While talking with her husband, I found that he was quite rational. His reason for talking to himself was that he was experiencing a serious legal problem, and the inner spiritual side of him criticized his outer words and actions. This quarrel set up a state of imbalance, which was resolved when he began to claim, "There is a Divine harmonious solution through the wisdom of the Infinite within me." As he adhered to this simple truth, he found in a short time that his prayer paid dividends. There was an amicable settlement out of court.

THE HEADLINES ANNOYED HIM

Talking with a man who had very high blood pressure, and who was on medication, the author learned that his complaint was that he would like to find inner peace, but that the articles in the morning newspaper vexed, annoyed, and irritated him beyond measure. He even allowed the headlines to disturb him.

I pointed out to him that it is true that the world goes from one crisis to another, but that it need not affect him personally. He began to perceive and understand that he as an individual could not prevent crime, mass murder, social upheavals, war, and disease, but that he could take charge of his own reactions and modify his attitude toward these happenings. There is no law that compels a man to get boiling mad because a newspaperman writes a sordid and morbid article.

The Bible says, *No man taketh it from me . . .* (John 10:18). The meaning is quite obvious that no man, news article, or circumstance, or condition can take away our peace or faith in God. We can give our peace away by giving up our control over our thoughts and emotions.

This man saw the point and decided then and there to let no article, news report, or happening rob him of his inner peace, poise, or serenity. When thoughts of fear, anger, or hate came to his mind, he immediately supplanted them by affirming, "God's peace fills my soul." He made a habit of that (and prayer is a good habit), and he eventually had the joy of hearing his doctor tell him to discontinue the medicine as his blood pressure was normal. In two weeks he had accomplished a state of inner peace and perfect composure.

BE FAITHFUL TO THE END

A few nights ago I gave a lecture at Dr. Bitzer's Church of Religious Science in Hollywood. The subject was, "The Wisdom of the I Ching."* After the lecture, an old friend who was present told me that her husband had been promised by his brother a sum of money and that he would send it immediately. This would have solved his acute financial problem. The letter was to be sent air mail, and he expected it in a few days. When he failed to receive the letter, though, he became terribly depressed and allowed despair to overwhelm him, which brought on an acute heart attack. The next day the letter arrived Special Delivery Air Mail.

He had permitted anxiety to control him. Had he remained quiet, still, and relaxed, trusting in the Divine Presence, he would have realized that the letter was on the way. When his wife showed him the letter and the contents, he

---

* See *Secrets of the I Ching* by Dr. Joseph Murphy, Parker Publishing Co., Inc., West Nyack, N.Y., 1970.

had a marvelous and rapid recovery. His physician said that his brother's letter was the best medicine. Remain faithful to the end, every step of the way. There is always an answer.

WEALTH IS IN YOU

I had a most interesting conversation with an oil man on the plane returning from a series of lectures at Unity Church in Phoenix, Arizona. He was what he termed an old-timer. His father had prospected for oil in Texas many years ago and had given up in disgust, saying there was no oil anywhere. He asked his son, "Why don't you try?" This oil man said that he went to the fields explored by his father and found oil, which netted him a small fortune over the years. His father had given up too soon.

The son's attitude was that God would guide him to the right place, and he discovered a profitable well in the same area where his father had explored. Wealth was in the mind of the son. It was also in the ground, but it took some intelligence and mental acumen to find it. He said to me that his Dad had a blind spot, since he was very jealous of his neighbors who had found oil and who had become rich. Looking through the eyes of jealousy and envy had blurred his father's vision, and he couldn't see the oil underneath his feet.

THE KINGDOM IS WITHIN YOU

The kingdom of intelligence, wisdom, and power is within you. In other words, God indwells you, and all the wisdom, guidance, power, and strength you need is instantly available to you. Your kingdom is an attitude of mind, a way of thinking, an emotional accent whereby you know you can achieve and overcome any challenge through the power of the Almighty within you. Make it a habit during every day to affirm frequently, "Divine peace fills my soul. Divine love governs all my activities. Divine right action is mine. Divine guidance is mine."

Make it a habit to pray as above and you will find peace and rest generated from the depths of yourself. Conditions, circumstances, people, the mountains, the lakes, or the sea will not by themselves give you peace of mind. The world is in constant turmoil, and this is why you go within and find and claim the peace that passeth understanding. Tune in with the Infinite, which lies stretched in smiling repose. Wonders will happen as you pray.

Overcoming the World

The Bible says: . . . *In the world ye shall have tribulation: but be of good cheer; I have overcome the world* (John 16:33). The world does not refer to material objects such as sticks and stones, trees and lakes. The world is the mass mind with its confusion, hate, jealousies, conflicts, dreams, and aspirations, the good and the bad, and wars and strife. In other words, it is the thinking, acting, and reacting of four billion people.

All of us are immersed in the mass mind, or law of averages. There is no use in getting excited, agitated, and perturbed about the conflicts in the world. Furthermore, you cannot run away from the world. You can rise above it by thinking spiritually, constructively, and harmoniously. Adopt an attitude of victory and triumph, and claim boldly: "God in the midst of me is guiding me, prospering me, and giving me strength and power to overcome." Radiate love and goodwill to all. Claim poise, balance, and equilibrium. As you claim these truths regularly, you will move through the maelstrom of this world's thinking into the experiences of satisfaction, contentment, and accomplishment.

SHE SAID, "I CAN'T STAND IT"

A young nurse said to me after the service at the Saddleback Theatre in Laguna Hills that she had received her first appointment in a medical clinic but that there were constant complaints, interruptions, strife, and contention. She was vexed and said to me, "The situation seems impossible. I can't stand it."

I suggested to her that it would do her no good to run away; that she was there to meet the challenges and difficulties and overcome them. Complaints, interruptions, contention, and upset people are a part of the job. She listened and decided to remain calm and affirm frequently, *"None of these things move me . . .* (Acts 20:24). I am here to conquer, to serve, to radiate love and understanding, and to gain experience."

She discovered that her changed attitude changed everything. She moves in the clinic now with a quiet mind. . . . *In quietness and in confidence shall be your strength . . .* (Isaiah 30:15). She discovered that the power of transcendence over turmoil and vexation was within herself. She found there was a power within her greater than any situation. . . . *Greater is he that is in you, than he that is in the world* (I John 4:4).

Everybody meets with difficulties, challenges, problems, strife, and contention as an inevitable part of experience here on earth; but the man or woman who realizes that every problem is Divinely outmatched wins victories and knows that joining up with the Infinite Presence and Power brings about the joy of the answered prayer. Your knowledge of the Divine Presence within you forms the basis of faith and peace of mind.

Be a Good Gardener

Your mind is the garden where you sow seeds, or thoughts, impressions, and beliefs. Your mind is called a vineyard in the Bible. The Bible deals with mental and spiritual laws under the guise and symbolism of physical and earthly things. Whatever we impress on our subconscious mind, good or bad, comes forth into our experience.

Man is forever blaming conditions, events, and circumstances rather than looking within himself and realizing that he becomes what he thinks all day long. Your health, happiness, and prosperity are not predicated upon events and actions of others but upon the way you think and feel. Your thought and feeling control your destiny. Remember, you are dealing with your own thoughts and your concept of yourself, which determine your future.

What Are You Projecting?

Recently I talked with a man who was projecting anger, resentment, and hostility to his associates, and they were responding with similar attitudes toward him. He did not know that he was at fault himself and was blaming them.

I explained to him that his mind was like a motion picture machine, which projects images on the screen. Accordingly, he reversed his attitude and began to silently exude goodwill, love, harmony, and peace toward all his associates and co-workers, and he discovered a different response. He perceived the cause within himself.

The Bible gives the answer in a beautiful way: *Judge not, that ye be not judged. For with what judgment ye judge, ye shall be judged* . . . (Matthew 7:1–2). . . . *With the same measure that ye mete withal it shall be measured to you again* (Luke 6:38). It is said, and rightly so, "Beauty is in the eye of the beholder." If your eyes are identified with the lovely, you will see only the lovely. *Unto the pure all things are pure* . . . (Titus 1:15).

Remember, you have the authority, the dominion, and the rulership over the government of your mind. You are the husbandman and the vineyard is your mind. Learn to possess your own mind and recall frequently that the treasure-house of Infinity is within you. Learn to lay hold of the vast potentialities of the Infinite within you and move forward into a greater measure of health, happiness, and peace of mind.

HE FOUND THE TREASURE HOUSE

A young man of ninety years, chronologically speaking, told me after the service on Sunday at the Saddleback Valley Plaza Theatre that he had discovered hidden talents he never knew he had. He began praying that Infinite Intelligence would reveal to him new creative ideas, which would bless and inspire people. He showed me some beautiful poetry which came forth freely from his pen. He is submitting these poems to various spiritual publications. They are, indeed, spiritual gems of wisdom.

As a young man he wandered all over the country doubting, questioning, fearing, grieving, hating, and fighting with others until, as he said, at the age of thirty, he discovered that life's greatest gifts were within himself and not in the fifty states of the Union. He is now living in Laguna Hills and contributing to the beauty and harmony of the area by giving of his wisdom and largess to all those around him.

LOOK WITHIN ALWAYS

Contemplate the Living Presence of God within you. Realize you live, move, and have your being in this Infinite Presence and Power. As you do this frequently, you will find yourself sustained, strengthened, and protected in all your ways. Spend some time every day contemplating things Divine. Remember, it is not running to and fro but accomplishment and achievement that counts.

Every morning when you arise, give thanks for your many

blessings and live in the joyous expectancy of the best, claiming it is the greatest day of your life because your Higher Self is revealing to you better ways to serve and grow spiritually. At night prior to sleep wrap yourself in the mantle of God's love, forgiving yourself for any errors of the day, and go off to sleep with the praise of God forever on your lips.

ARE YOU READY?

In a recent lecture I used the statement, "All things be ready if our mind be so." Shakespeare here points out a great truth dealing with mental and spiritual laws. A young lady present wrote me and said that she had never heard it explained before and that it applied to her. She had been constantly postponing marriage, since she felt she was not ready because she had been looking after her parents. Suddenly, she came to the conclusion, "I am ready now." She phoned the young man who wanted to marry her, and the author had the privilege of performing the ceremony.

You can be and you can do what you want to be and do if you are mentally ready. Your great opportunity in life is really your mental acceptance and readiness. This young woman's parents were not a stumbling block to her fulfillment in life. This was a blind spot in her own mind. Her parents were delighted, and they hired a nurse and a maid to help them in their home, which actually proved to be a far better arrangement for all concerned. When love comes into your life, it contributes to the peace and happiness of all those around you and all people everywhere.

Remember a simple truth: Whenever you are mentally ready, you will find that everything else is also ready. In the early days of America, the Pilgrims could have used the telephone, radio, automobile, cinemas, airplanes, etc., but they were not mentally ready. They believed that the horse and buggy was the only means of transportation. Moses, Elijah, Buddha, and all the ancient teachers could have used radio and television to dramatize and portray the great truths of life had they been mentally receptive and ready.

The laws of nature never vary, however, and were the same then as now, but the minds of the ancient seers and prophets were not ready for these inventions. Supply and demand are one, but you must supply mental readiness and the answer will then come to you in Divine order.

PUTTING GOD FIRST

Recently I conducted a memorial service for a man who was 104 years old. His widow said that as far as she could recall, he had never been sick, but the night prior to his transition, though, he had told her that he was going on to meet his loved ones. He then passed on in his sleep. His widow said that every morning of his life he had read out loud the 91st Psalm, emphasizing the phrase, . . . *With long life will I satisfy him* . . . (Psalm 91:16). He emphasized the following statement also: *Thou wilt shew me the path of life* . . . (Psalm 16:11). *Keep thy heart with all diligence; for out of it are the issues of life* (Proverbs 4:23).

Life to this man meant a life of happiness, achievement,

and usefulness. He enjoyed life and gave of his talents in a wonderful way. The long life spoken of in the Bible is a long period of joy, freedom, peace, and accomplishment. The abundant life comes to all when they keep and practice the Golden Rule and put God first in their lives.

SHE WAS USING THE OUIJA BOARD

I receive many letters from men and women who live in different states, claiming that they hear voices at night shouting obscenities and vulgarities in their ears, as well as all kinds of profane language. One woman wrote saying that an entity had been telling her to commit suicide and join him in the next dimension.

She had been using the Ouija Board and lived in constant fear that some evil entity would take over. What she continually feared finally came upon her. She did not know that her subconscious mind accepts all kinds of suggestions, good or bad, and that her fear of an evil entity was a constant command to her subconscious mind, which responded and played the role of an evil spirit. Actually, it was her own subconscious mind talking back to her.

I gave her the following prayer, which is very effective, telling her to repeat this prayer aloud many times, day or night, as often as needed, and she would feel the Presence of God. This awareness will dethrone from one's mind all negative influences that are bothersome. Make it real, affirm these truths, and boldly assert:

"I mean this and I decree it. God lives in me. God talks and walks in me. My life is God's life, and God's peace fills my mind and heart. God's love saturates my soul. I am growing in wisdom, truth, and beauty. I am whole, I am strong, I am happy, joyous, and free. I can do all things through the God-Power which strengtheneth me. I know that whatever I attach to 'I AM,' I become. God careth for me. I am surrounded by the sacred circle of God's eternal love. The whole armor of God surrounds me. God is guiding me. His light shines in me."

Following this spiritual meditation, she was to issue this command to her subconscious mind boldly, incisively, and decisively: "I decree you to get out now. I mean this. I am sincere. Get thee hence. God is here now. Wherever God is, there is no evil. Be thou gone. I am free."

Following this technique, she became completely free in two weeks' time, and she no longer dabbles with the Ouija Board.

LAY HOLD OF THIS KEY

The Bible says, . . . *I AM THAT I AM* . . . (Exodus 3:14), which means unconditioned Being—the Living Spirit Almighty. It is a nameless name. It means the Only Presence and Power—God. It is an attempt by Moses to express the Infinite Nature of God, which is without face, form, or figure. It is timeless, ageless, and formless.

"I AM" means you are announcing the Presence of God in you. You are an individualization of the Infinite. If you say,

"I AM John Jones," you are announcing that you are a man possessing a certain name, nationality, characteristics, position in life, etc. In other words, you are the Universal Life appearing in the form of man. Whatever you attach to "I AM" you become.

Use this affirmation and feel the truth of what you affirm: "I AM whole, strong, powerful, loving, prosperous, successful, illumined, and inspired." Make it a habit to reiterate these truths and you will have found the key which unlocks the treasure house within you.

THE FIRST AND THE LAST

In a recent Bible class on the inner meaning of the Book of Revelation, a man asked the meaning of . . . *I am Alpha and Omega, the first and the last* . . . (Revelation 1:11).

He was a businessman, and I explained it along these lines: I AM is the Presence of God in all of us. It is the unconditioned consciousness or awareness. It is the only Presence and Power and is the Cause of all manifestation. It is Omnipresent and the very Life of all of us. The individual I AM is the universal I AM conditioned by man's thinking and beliefs. It is our personal consciousness, which means the way we think, feel, and believe as well as to whatever we give our mental consent.

He began to see what the Bible meant by the statement *I AM the first and the last*, the beginning and the end, for our own consciousness is the beginning of every enterprise or undertaking. Our actions, experiences, and results are secondary.

We may begin writing a book, which takes some time; then it comes to an end when finished. The same would apply to any invention, discovery, or business. The beginning was in the mind of the person. If he began or started his new business with faith and confidence, the end, or result, would end up as a successful enterprise. The end would agree with the beginning.

This man said that he began making picture postal cards of a religious nature with great love in his heart, and he received loving letters from nearly everyone to whom he sent them. His present wife received one of the cards, and that is how his loved one came into his life.

Begin your business with faith and confidence and you will win success. The beginning and the end are the same. Your thought and feeling is the beginning, and the result is the end.

SHE FAILED THREE TIMES

A real estate saleswoman said she had opened a different office three times and had failed miserably. She went to church, received the sacraments, and prayed regularly for prosperity and success. The explanation was the cure for this saleslady. She feared failure and expected to fail. She had a mental picture of failure. Her constant negativity undermined all her work. She attracted clients and opportunities came her way, but the pattern of failure persisted. Since she began with thoughts of failure, the result coincided with the beginning.

She learned to reverse her mental attitude and enthroned

in her mind the pattern of success by affirming every morning and night: "Infinite Spirit attracts to me clients who have the money to buy and who want the homes I have for sale. They are blessed and prospered, and I AM likewise blessed and prospered. I AM a tremendous success in all my undertakings. I AM born to win and succeed in life. I know that when I begin with the idea of success, the end will be successful."

When fear thoughts came to her, she supplanted them immediately by affirming, "Success is mine. It is wonderful." She made a habit of this, and since the subconscious is the seat of habit, she is now compelled to succeed and is moving onward and upward.

YOUR MOOD IS CONTAGIOUS

Everyone knows the workman or salesgirl who is sour, cynical, and full of criticism of others and about everything else in general. This negative attitude is picked up subconsciously by others, and they find themselves in a daily rut, never moving up in the ladder of life. Many are bitter and jealous of those who have gone up the ladder of life. This mood of jealousy and envy robs them of life's energy, and they are always tired, exhausted, and lethargic.

Warm, kind, understanding, and outgoing people release the healing power of life, and they pour out the sunshine of Divine love into their works.

Be a Good Boss

You become a good boss when you cease blaming your environment, your early childhood, your parents, and your inheritance. It is no use blaming others; the cause lies in your own thought and feeling. There is no one to change but yourself.

Learn to take control and be boss over your thoughts, feelings, actions, and reactions. Realize that you are a king over your own household. Claim that Divine law and order govern you at all times. Begin to think, speak, act, and react from the standpoint of the Divine Center within you. You can order your thoughts around and tell them where to direct their attention. See to it that all your thoughts pay you dividends in health, success, good human relations, and in all other phases of your life.

The man who refuses to take charge of his own thoughts will be bossed and controlled by conditions, circumstances, and people. He finds himself pushed around and coerced and controlled by the mass mind. Choose your own thoughts based on Divine principles and eternal verities, and all your ways will be pleasantness and all your paths will be peaceful.

Good Fortune

Recently I talked with a man eighty years old, who told me that his maxim all his life had been: "I expect good fortune." And he has had good fortune all his life. His mother, who was a Quaker, told him when he was very young: "John, always expect good fortune and you will have it." This is wise

254 Within You Is the Power

advice, because all of us get what we expect out of life and not what we want.

Believe in good fortune and you shall experience good along all lines, because the law of life is the law of belief.

Know Who You Are

The Bible says: *A bastard shall not enter into the congregation of the Lord; even to his tenth generation shall he not enter into the congregation of the Lord* (Deuteronomy 23:2). "Our Father" mentioned in the Bible means the Life Principle, which is the Progenitor or Father of us all. We are all brothers and sisters and are intimately related to one another.

Every man should know the Source from which he springs. The Bible deals with psychology and metaphysics and speaks in metaphors, similes and parables. We must see the hidden meaning. When a man does not know that God, or Infinite Intelligence, indwells him, he is unable to meet life's challenges in the right way. He fails to see that there is a wisdom and power within him, enabling him to solve all problems and to rise triumphantly and express himself at the highest level.

If a man looks at his human ancestors as the source of his being, he is indeed limiting himself and will feel restricted and circumscribed by his environment, upbringing, and limited beliefs of his forebears. Knowing that God is his real Father and that he has inherited all the powers, qualities, and attributes of the Infinite gives him the feeling and the awareness that he can do great things, and he will go forth conquering and to conquer.

To take the passage from Deuteronomy literally would be absurd, but when a man knows his true Source and tunes in with the Infinite, he rejects completely the illusions, false beliefs, and superstitions of the masses and becomes master of his environment and conditions. Man comes of royal lineage, for his Father is God, and God is Spirit; and, as Emerson says, "Every spirit builds itself a house." Then he is in complete charge and molds and fashions his own destiny.

. . . And as thou hast believed, so be it done unto thee . . . (Matthew 8:13).

ABOUT THE AUTHOR

A native of Ireland who resettled in America, **Joseph Murphy**, Ph.D., D.D., (1898–1981) was a prolific and widely admired New Thought minister and writer, best known for his metaphysical classic *The Power of Your Subconscious Mind*, an international bestseller since it first appeared on the self-help scene in 1963. A popular speaker, Murphy lectured on both American coasts and in Europe, Asia, and South Africa. His many books and pamphlets on the auto-suggestive and metaphysical faculties of the human mind have entered multiple editions—some of the most poignant of which appear in this volume. Murphy is considered one of the pioneering voices of affirmative-thinking philosophy.